Dictionary of
Mysticism

Dictionary of
Mysticism

edited by

Frank Gaynor

The Citadel Press   Secaucus, New Jersey

Second paperbound printing, 1973
Copyright © 1953 by Philosophical Library, Inc.
Published by Citadel Press
A division of Lyle Stuart Inc.
120 Enterprise Avenue, Secaucus, N.J. 07094
In Canada: George J. McLeod Limited
73 Bathurst St., Toronto 2B, Ontario
Manufactured in the United States of America
ISBN 0-8065-0172-3

Dictionary of Mysticism

Aaron's rod: The rod, or wand, with a serpent twined round it, which was used in the Mosaic ceremony of initiation; it appears to have contained the sacred fire. Now commonly employed as an emblem signifying a physician; similar to the caduceus of Hermes.

Abbadon: The Hebrew name of the "bottomless pit," the place of the lost in *Sheol;* the abyss of hell.

ABC of the Devil: Handwritten books for the use of magicians and sorcerers.

Abhasa: A Sanskrit term (literally meaning *shining forth*) for the cosmopsychological process which takes place as the One becomes the Many, as it is described by the philosophical system called *Trika* (q.v.).

Abhasana: The same as *abhasa* (q.v.).

Abhava: Sanskrit for *non-being, non-existence.* In Hindu philosophy, a means of correct knowledge defined as the deduction of the existence of one of two opposite things from the non-existence of the other.

Abheda: A Sanskrit term (literally meaning *indistinct*) for *identity*, used especially in reference to any philosophy which denies the distinctness of spiritual and material, or divine and human principles.

Abhiseka: In Hinduism, the ceremonial bathing in sacred waters. In Buddhism, the tenth stage of perfection. The term is used also for the anointment of kings and high officials upon their ascension to power or as a recognition of some signal achievement.

Abidharma: The third part of the Buddhist Tripitaka (q.v.) containing lessons in metaphysics and occultism.

Abigor: In demonography, the name of a powerful demon, high-ranking in the infernal empire.

Abominable snowmen: A legendary race of superhuman giants, hostile to man, inhabiting the snowy slopes of the Himalayas.

Abracadabra: A magic word. A triangular arrangement of its letters worn on an amulet is believed by occultists to bring health and ward off disease.

Abraxas: A magic word, said to be the name of a god, the seven letters of which form the number 365, the number of days in a year. The word engraved on a gem or stone is considered by occultists to constitute a very potent charm.

Absent treatment: Cure of physical illness from a distance, by occult or metaphysical means.

Absolute: In metaphysics and mystic philosophy, the Absolute is the ultimate referent of thought, the Unconditioned, the opposite of the Relative.

Absolute Ego: In the philosophical system of J .G. Fichte (1762-1814), the Ego before its differentiation into an empirical Self and Non-Self.

Absolutism: The theory of the *Absolute* (q.v.); the view that standards of moral value are objective, absolute, superhuman and eternal.

Abstract: A partial aspect or quality considered in isolation from an object as a whole.

Acarya: A Sanskrit word, meaning "spiritual teacher"; a title given to high-ranking adepts of esoteric science.

Accepted chela: A disciple of esoteric philosophy, who has passed the *fourth initiation*.

Acolyte: In occultism, "anyone under occult discipline at a stage of first responsibilities, but prior to formal induction into the invisible fellowship; a licentiate or probationer." (Marc Edmund Jones)

Acosmism: The doctrine that the external, physical world is non-existent, unreal, a mere appearance (*maya*) of the Supreme Being, who is the only reality.

Active influence: A term used in astrology, to denote the influence resulting from an aspect between two or more astrological factors or sensitive points, thereby producing the action that can materialize in an event.

Activism: The philosophical theory which considers activity, particularly spiritual activity, to be the essence of reality. The concept of pure act (*actus purus*) traceable to Aristotle's conception of divinity, was influential in Scholastic thought, and persists in Leibniz, Fichte and modern idealism.

Adam Kadmon: Hebrew for *primeval man*. The Kabalistic name representing humanity, the "Heavenly Man," prior to falling into sin.

Adamic: An alternative name for the Polarian *root race* (q.v.).

Adamic era: See: *Cosmic epochs.*

Adapa: In Babylonian mythology, the name of a hero created and endowed with wisdom by Ea, whose temple at Eridu he was to tend. Summoned before Anu, god of the sky, he unwittingly refused immortality.

Additor: A modified ouija board; a small round, hollow box, with a pointer protruding from it, moves under the fingers over the board bearing the letters of the alphabet.

Adept: One who has attained to proficiency in any art or science. In occultism, one who has attained the stage of initiation and has become a Master of esoteric science and philosophy.

Adhyatma: Sanskrit for *Supreme Spirit.*

Adience: That continuous, automatic repetition of action which esoteric philosophy regards as a characteristic of an *elemental* (q.v.).

Aditi: The name (Sanskrit for *boundlessness*) of a Vedic goddess, mother of the gods known as *Adityas*; she is identified at times with the earth, at times with the sky, and at other times is hailed as a cow.

Adityas: A group of Vedic gods, sons of the goddess *Aditi.* Their number is variously given as six or eight, in later times also as twelve.

Admadiya: A Moslem sect founded in the late 19th century in India, which interprets the *jihad* (q.v.) as a striving after righteousness.

Adonai: Hebrew word, meaning *The Lord,* used by Jews in speech and in writing instead of the name Jehovah, the mystic name of the God of Israel, which must not be pronounced.

Adoption: The acquisition of a status or position.

Adoptive masonry: Comasonry (q.v.).

Adramelech: In demonography, the president of the Supreme Council of the infernal empire.

Advaita: Sanskrit for *non-dualism*. The Vedantic doctrine of monism advocated by Samkara, which contends that only the Ultimate Principle (*Brahman*) has any actual existence, and that all phenomenal existence is an illusion (*maya*).

Advanced soul: In occult philosophy, a human being whose spiritual development has exceeded that attainable by his fellow-men.

Adventists: Religious sects originating from the Advent Movement, professing the personal and premillennial second advent of Christ, and the renewal of the Earth as an abode for the redeemed after a physical resurrection of the dead.

Aegir: The sea god of Norse mythology.

Aeromancy: Divination by observing atmospheric conditions or ripples on the surface of the water.

Aesculapius: The Roman god of healing and medicine.

Aesir: In Norse mythology, the entourage of Odin.

Aesma: The evil spirit of wrath, inspirer of vengeance and evil, in Zoroastrian demonology.

Aeviternity: Eternity regarded as a whole, distinct from the flux of time—an endless temporal medium in which events and objects are fixed relative to each other.

Afreet: A class of jinns (q.v.) in Arabic mythology. (Also referred to as *afrit, afrite* or *efreet*).

Agamas: The canon of scriptures of Jainism.

Agathodemon: Greek for *good demon*. A beneficent nature spirit or minor deity.

Ages of mankind: See: *Root race*.

Agla: The combination of the first letters of four Hebrew words meaning "Thou art forever mighty, O Lord." Used as a magic word to exorcise demons and evil spirits.

Agni: The Vedic god of fire.

Agnosticism: The belief that certain knowledge has not been attained, either in some particular field (usually the religious) or in any and all fields of supposed knowledge.

Agricultural astrology: An application of astrology to the planting and the harvesting of crops.

Aham brahma asmi: Sanskrit for "I am *brahman,*" the formula of the Upanishad, denoting the full coincidence of the human and divine, arrived at not so much by a spontaneous mystic insight as by logical deduction from the nature of world and self.

Ahamkara: A Sanskrit term (literally meaning *I-maker*) used to designate the principle which generates man's consciousness of his own ego or personal identity.

Ahanta: A Sanskrit term (literally meaning *I-hood* or *selfness*) for the state of being an Ego.

Ahimsa: Sanskrit for *non-injuring, not killing.* The Hindu doctrine of the oneness and sacredness of all life, human and animal.

Ain Soph: See: *En-Soph.*

Ahriman: In Zoroastrian mythology, the personified principle of evil, leader of the Devas, powers of evil, in eternal conflict with Ahura Mazda. (Also called *Angra Mainyu.*)

Ahura: In Zoroastrian terminology, a beneficent deity.

Ahura Mazda: Literally *Lord of Knowledge.* The chief benevolent deity of Zoroastrianism, personification of the Good, leader of the powers of light.

Akasha: In occultism, a celestial ether, or astral light that fills all space. According to occult teaching, every thought and action which takes place in the material world, is recorded in this akashic medium, whereby one possessed of psychic vision can read and translate the panorama of history, the *Akashic Records.* They also hint that some day science will be able to tap this record and thus draw upon and even re-enact the words and actions of past ages. (Also spelled *Akasa.*)

Akashic: Of or pertaining to the *akasha* (q.v.).

Akashic Records: Scenic representations of every action, sentiment and thought since the beginning of the world. (Cf. *Akasha.*)

Aksara: Sanskrit for *imperishable*; a descriptive synonym for *brahman* (q.v.), the Absolute, in the Upanishads; it has also the meaning of "syllable."

Alam: Arabic for *world*. In Sufi terminology, the seven cosmic planes called *alam* are: 1) the lowest one, *alam i sugrah*, the world of human experience; 2) *alam i nasut*, the material world of forms and bodies; 3) *alam i mithal*, the astral world; 4) *alam i malakut*, the spiritual world; 5) *alam i kabrut*, the radiant plane of divine splendor; 6) *alam i lahut*, the exalted divine plane of the first emanation; 7) the highest, *alam i hahut*, plane of absolute inactual being.

Alastor: In demonography, the name of a cruel, evil demon.

Alaya: The World Soul (q.v.).

Alcahest: See: *Alkahest*.

Alchemist: A practitioner of alchemy (q.v.) in any or all of its aspects.

Alchemy: The science of decomposing and recomposing things, as well as of changing their essential nature and raising it higher— transmuting them into each other. While chemistry deals with lifeless matter, alchemy employs life as a factor, and deals with higher forces of nature and the conditions of matter under which they operate. In its lowest aspect, it deals with physical substances, but in its highest aspect it teaches the regeneration of the spiritual man, the purification of mind, will and thought, and the ennobling of all the faculties of the human soul.

Alecto: In Roman mythology, one of the Furies (q.v.), genius of pestilence, war and vengeance.

Alectorius: In occultism, a small stone said to be found in the innards of cocks, and to have the effects of a powerful magical charm.

Aleph: The first letter of the Hebrew alphabet. The most sacred of the Hebrew letters; seldom pronounced because indicative of the Deity.

Alfheim: The dwelling place of the elves of Norse mythology.

Alkahest: The universal solvent sought by alchemists. Materially, a substance capable of dissolving all other material substance, reducing it to the original matter of which it was formed. Symbolically, a force capable of affecting the astral forms of all things and of dissolving them by changing the polarity of their molecules.

All Hallow's Eve: An ancient Druidic festival when all fires had to be extinguished, except for the sacred altar fires of the Druid priests.

Allegorical interpretation: The interpretation of a book, a saying, a ritual, etc., discovering a hidden, symbolic, spiritual, occult or metaphorical meaning in it.

Allegory: Description in symbolical terms, or representation in symbolical form, with the true meaning hidden beneath the literal or obvious significance.

Allmuseri: An African occult society.

Alocer: In demonography, the name of a mighty demon.

Alphitomancy: An ancient form of divination of the guilt or innocence of an accused individual by making him swallow a piece of a barley loaf, which was supposed to produce indigestion in the guilty.

Alpiel: In Hebrew mysticism, a demon who rules over fruit-trees.

Alraune: In Teutonic mythology, a female demon. Also the name of small statuettes made of ash root and supposed to have magic powers.

Altar: Any place set aside for communicating with a god, with supernatural entities, or with the dead, by means of sacrifices or offerings.

Amaimon: In magic lore, the spirit ruling the Eastern portion of the universe.

Amazons: A mythical race of warrior women who lived in a matriarchal society and put their male children to death, raising only the girls to become warriors.

Ambrosia: The food of the gods of Greek mythology.

Amen: A Hebrew word, used nowadays in the meaning "verily," but considered by occultists to have originally been a mystic word, related to the Sanskrit *om*. In theosophical and related esoteric parlance, *amen* means "the concealed."

Ameretat: In Zoroastrianism, one of the Amesha Spentas (q.v.), the personified representation of immortality, spirit of trees and plants.

Amesha Spenta: One of the six immortal holy ones, high deities of Zoroastrianism, attendants of Ahura Mazda. They represent the personified attributes of Ahura Mazda: Ameretat (immortality), Aramaiti (holy harmony), Asha (righteousness), Haurvatat (saving health), Kshathra (rulership), and Vohumanah (good thought). They are known also as the Amshaspands.

Amica: The Aquarian Mystical Institute of Color Awareness. (Cf. *color awareness*.)

Amon: In demonography, the name of one of the strongest of all demons.

Amon; Ammon: Originally a local god of Thebes in ancient Egypt, later identified with Amon-Ra (q.v.).

Amon-Ra: The Egyptian king of the gods, creator of the universe; originally the god of Thebes, later supreme god of all Egypt.

A.M.O.R.C.: The abbreviation of the full, official name of the Rosicrucian Order (q.v.), i.e.: *Ancient Mystical Order Rosae Crucis.*

Amor Dei intellectualis: Latin for *intellectual love of God.* A term introduced by Spinoza, which he uses to denote an enduring, impersonal love.

Amrita: The drink or food of the gods of the Vedic myths. Identified with the *soma* drink (q.v.).

Amshaspands: The six Amesha Spentas of Zoroastrianism.

Amulet: A material object on which a charm is written or over which a charm was said, worn on the person to protect the wearer against dangers, disease, to serve as a shield against demons, ghosts, evil magic, and to bring luck and good fortune.

Amy: In demonography, the name of a mighty demon, one of the ruling hierarchy of the infernal empire.

An: The Sumerian god of heaven.

Analogy: A similitude in relationship.

Anamelech: In demonography, the name of a demon, harbinger of bad tidings.

Anamnesis: Greek for *recollection.* Plato used this term for the memory which human consciousness has of facts and events in an earlier incarnation.

Ananda: Sanskrit for *joy, happiness, bliss.*

Ananisapta: In occultism, a word of magical effects; when written on parchment and worn on the body, it is believed to be a protection against disease.

Ananya bhakti: In *bhakti yoga* (q.v.) the cult of the transcendent but objective monotheistic God.

Anastikaya: A Sanskrit term meaning *not body-like, unextended.* (Cf. *astikaya.*)

Ancestor worship: A religious system based on the belief that the spirits of the dead linger about their earthly habitations, have powers of protecting and blessing those responsible for their care, and of avenging their neglect. The doctrine and practice is observed and followed in various parts of the world, notably in China and Japan.

Anchoret; anchorite: Greek for *recluse.* The term applied to an extreme type of Christian ascetics who sought spiritual perfection by withdrawing from the community, often exposing themselves to hardships.

Ancient Mystical Order Rosae Crucis: See: *Rosicrucian Order.*

Ancilia: The twelve sacred shields of ancient Rome, on the safety of which the fate of the Roman people was believed to depend. The first Ancile was said to have dropped to earth from heaven.

Android: A human being produced by means other than natural conception and birth.

Angakok: An Eskimo shamanistic medium and witch-doctor.

Angel: A living creature of the spirit world, intermediate between gods and humans, and either friendly or hostile toward humanity. Angels belong to the class properly known as *demons.* In the monotheistic religions, the word *angel* is usually applied to the benevolent agents and messengers of God.

Angelified flesh: The heavenly substance of which the bodies of angels are formed, according to Christian mystics.

Angelology: The study and classification of angels and their characteristics.

Angra Mainyu: An alternative name of Ahura Mazda (q.v.).

Anima mundi: Latin for *soul of the world.* See: *World Soul.*

Animal magnetism: According to all schools of mysticism, occultism and esoteric philosophy, a force which causes a fluid emanation to issue forth from all men, animals and even inanimate objects as an *aura* (q.v.) or as a form of light; some persons can emit it, for purposes of magic healing, from their eyes or the tips of their fingers.

Animal soul: In occult terminology, the personalized desire in man.

Animatism: The belief that all or certain important objects possess life or communicable energy. The belief in an impersonal supernatural power.

Animism: The belief in spirits of nature. The belief that persons and objects are animated by spirits. Also, the belief that all or most of animate beings as well as all or most of inanimate nature possess reason and will equal to those of man and have human-like mental processes.

Ankh: The Egyptian cross, shaped like a capital T with an oval loop on the top, symbol of life in occult tradition.

Annakaya: Sanskrit for *physical body*.

Anointing tablet: In ancient Egyptian occult practices, a device entombed with the bodies or mummies of the deceased; an alabaster tablet containing seven hollows for the seven holy oils intended for magical protection on the journey to the next world.

Anpiel: In Hebrew mysticism, the angel ruling the birds.

Antahkarana: A Sanskrit term, literally meaning *internal sense organ*. In occult philosophy, the term is used to indicate the bridge between the higher and the lower aspect of the *manas*.

Antediluvian: Before the Deluge.

Anthropomancy: The ancient art of divination by examining the intestines of a dead person—specifically, of a human sacrifice.

Anthropomorphic: Of human shape; conceived of as shaped like human beings.

Anthropomorphism: The ascription of human traits or characteristics to non-human entities, or representing them in human form.

Anthropopathism: The ascription of human feelings to non-human beings or objects.

Anthroposcopy: The deduction of a person's character, characteristics, abilities, etc. from his face.

Anthroposophy: An occult and mystic philosophical movement, based on the teachings of its founder, Rudolf Steiner, aiming at man's progressive liberation from the chains of egoism and at the development of his dormant faculties and higher capacities for knowledge and enlightenment, to enable him to perceive and respond to "subtler manifestations of Nature." Anthroposophists place great emphasis, among other things, on the occult significance of colors and their relations to human emotions (cf. *color awareness*).

Antichrist: The enemy of mankind who will establish a reign of evil in the world, as a punishment for man's wickedness. His reign, replete with wars, evil doings and miracles of black magic, will last for fifty years, but he will be overthrown by Christ at His second coming.

Antipathy: In astrology, a term denoting disharmony of two bodies, usually planets, which rule or are exalted in opposite Signs. (For example, Saturn ruling Capricorn, has an antipathy for the Moon, ruling Cancer.)

Anu; Anum: The Babylonian and Assyrian god of heaven, ruler of destiny, king of gods, chief of the Babylonian triad of gods (the other two were Ea and Enlil).

Anubis: The jackal-headed god of ancient Egypt, son of Osiris; he presides over the embalming of the dead, leads them to the hall of judgment and supervises the weighing of their hearts.

Anugita: An occult treatise, one of the *Upanishads*.

Anugraham: Sanskrit for *grace*.

Anwyl: The world of the dead in Celtic mythology.

Apantomancy: Divination by means of any object that happens to meet the eye.

Apeiron: Greek for *infinite, indeterminate*. The Greek philosopher Anaximander (6th century B.C.) used the term for the primal indeterminate matter out of which all things come to be.

Apheta: In astrology, the planet or place that exercises an influence over the life and death of the native (q.v.).

Aphrodite: Greek goddess of love and beauty.

Apis: The bull-headed god of ancient Egypt, regarded as an incarnation of Osiris. Also, a black bull with distinctive markings, whose worship was linked with various deities.

Apocatastasis: Greek for *re-establishment*. In Stoic philosophy, the belief that all things will return to their original condition after a cycle of ages.

Apollo: The Roman god, son of Jupiter, known by many names, principally as Sol (the sun).

Apotropaism: Protective or defensive magic, i.e., the use of magic rituals, incantations or other esoteric formulae in order to ward off or to overcome evil influences.

Apparition: A supernormal appearance; especially in spiritualistic and mediumistic practices.

Apport: The arrival of an object through solid matter; also, the object so appearing.

Appulse: In astrology, the near approach of one orbital body to another—a conjunction; the culmination at or crossing of the meridian. (Applied particularly to the appulse of the Moon to the Earth's shadow.)

Aquarian Epoch: The era of the world which, according to occult teachings, began in March 1948, when the sun entered the constellation of Aquarius and the previous era, called the Piscean Epoch, ended. The Aquarian Epoch is to last 2,000 years. Many esoteric societies and organizations have therefore names containing the word Aquarian, e.g., the Aquarian Order, the Aquarian Mission, the Aquarian Mystical Institute of Color Awareness, etc.

Aquarius (The Water Bearer): The eleventh sign of the zodiac. Its symbol ($\approx$) represents a stream of water, symbolizing the servant of humanity who pours out the water of knowledge to quench the thirst of the world. The Sun is in Aquarius annually from January 21 to February 20. Astrologically it is the second thirty-degree arc following the Sun's passing of the Winter Solstice, occupying a position along the Ecliptic from 300° to 330°. It is the "fixed" quality of the element Air, in which the will is largely motivated by reasoning processes—whether sound or unsound. It is positive, hot, moist, sanguine, rational and obeying. Ruler: Saturn; or by some moderns: Uranus. Exaltation: Mercury. Detriment: Sun. Symbolic interpretation: Waves, or water, or the vibrationary waves of electricity; parallel lines of force.

Aquastor: In occultism, a being created by the power of imagination and concentration of thought.

Aralu: The underworld, abode of the dead in Babylonian mythology. Conceived of as a vast, dark underground cave, entered through a hole in the earth, guarded by seven doors, to which all human beings go after death, never to return, but able to communicate with and give oracles to the living.

Aramaiti: One of the six Amesha Spentas (q.v.) of Zoroastrianism, the personified representation of holy harmony, spirit of the earth.

Arambha-vada: The theory of evolution taught by the Indian philosophical systems Nyaya and Vaisesika, stating that atoms combine upon being created to form the world in its entirety.

Aranyakas: The "Forest Books" of Hinduism, so called because they were used in teachings in the secrecy of the forest; they are mystical, esoteric meditations on the meaning of ritual lore.

Arariel: In Hebrew mysticism, the angel who presides over the waters.

Arathron: The Olympian Spirit (q.v.) governing Saturn, ruler of 49 Olympian Provinces of the universe; his day is Saturday.

Arbatel: A book of magic rituals, published in the late sixteenth century.

Arcane: A synonym for *esoteric* or *occult*.

Arcanum: An elixir used as a stimulant for divination. (Plural: *arcana*. Cf. *tarot*.)

Arcanum arcanorum: Medieval Latin term for the "secret of secrets"; the ultimate secret.

Archaes: A synonym for *astral light* (q.v.).

Archer: See: *Sagittarius.*

Archetypal world: See: *Yesod.*

Archetype: The original pattern, of which actual things are copies or reproductions. A collective, generalized representative of an idea or group of ideas or characteristics.

Architect: See: *Sovereign Grand Architect of the Universe.*

Archons: In occultism, primordial planetary spirits. In Manicheism, the Sons of Dark, who swallowed up the bright elements of the Primal Man.

Arda Viraf Nameh: A sacred book of Zoroastrianism, dealing with cosmogony, cosmology and eschatology.

Ares: The ancient Greek god of war and pestilence. The Romans identified him with Mars.

Ariel: The poetic name of Jerusalem used by Hebrew mystics.

Aries (The Ram): The first sign of the zodiac. Its symbol

(♈) represents the head and horns of the ram. In astrology, it is a symbol of offensive power—a weapon of the gods, hence an implement of the will. The Babylonians sacrificed rams during the period when the Sun occupied this sign, which occurs annually from March 21 to April 20. Astrologically and astronomically it is the first thirty-degree arc beginning at the point of the Spring Equinox. It is the "leading" quality of the element Fire: positive, diurnal, movable, dry, hot, fiery, choleric and violent. Ruler: Mars. Exaltation: Sun. Detriment: Venus. Fall: Saturn. Symbolic interpretation: Sprouting seed; fire in eruption; a fountain of water; a ram's horns.

Aries era: See: *Cosmic epochs.*

Arioch: In demonology, the name of a demon of vengeance.

Ariolist: A practitioner of the ancient art of divination by altars, called *ariolatio.*

Arithmancy: Fortune-telling by numbers, especially by the number of letters in names. (Also called *arithmomancy.*)

Artificial omen: A sign of future events which will or may happen as an act of human doing or will.

Aruspicy: An ancient method of divination by examining the entrails of human or animal sacrifices. (Also called *haruspicy.*)

Aryasatyani: The *Four Noble Truths* (q.v.) taught by Gautama Buddha.

Aryan: The fifth *root race* (q.v.) in esoteric philosophy.

Asana: Sanskrit for *sitting, posture;* one of the stages of the practice of Yoga.

Ascendant: In astrology, the degree of the Zodiac (q.v.) which appeared on the eastern horizon at the moment for which a Figure (q.v.) is to be cast.

Ascending arc: In theosophical occultism, the ascent of the evolving *monads* (q.v.) from the physical plane or globe upwards through the higher levels of existence. (Also called *luminous arc.*)

Ascension: In astrology, the vertical rising of a planet above the ecliptic, equator or horizon. *Right Ascension* is the circle of declination reckoned toward the east from 0° Aries, measured in the plane of the Equator. *Oblique Ascension* is measured on the Prime Vertical.

Asceticism: The view that the physical body is an evil and a detriment to a righteous moral and spiritual life, and that through moderation or renunciation of the things generally considered pleasant, one can reach a higher spiritual state or degree of enlightenment. Also, the practice of this belief.

Aseka: Sanskrit for *adept* (q.v.)

Asgard: In Norse mythology, Odin's headquarters, home of the gods, also housing the Valhalla, hall of the chosen among those slain in battle.

Asha: In Zoroastrianism, one of the six Amesha Spentas (q.v.), personified representation of righteousness, spirit of fire.

Ashram: The Hindu name of a settlement of disciples living with or around a *guru* (spiritual leader or teacher).

Ashtart: The fertility goddess of the Semitic races; ever-virginal, yet the fruitful mother and creator of life. Also known as Astarte, in Babylonia as Ishtar, and in Canaan as Ashtoreth.

Ashtavadhaza: In Hindu mysticism, the ability to grasp or attend to different matters at the same time.

Ashur: A national war god of ancient Assyria, represented shooting the bow inside of a winged disk.

Asmita: A Sanskrit term meaning *"I-am-ness."* The view which presumes lower states of mind to be the Self (*purusha*).

Asmodeus: In demonography, a destructive demon, at times identified with the serpent of the Garden of Eden, also with Samael (q.v.).

Asomatic: A Greek term, meaning *disembodied* (separated from the body).

Aspect: In occultism and esotericism, the form under which any natural or mystic principle manifests itself.

Aspect: In astrology, certain angular relationships between the rays which reach the Earth from two celestial bodies, or between one ray and a given point; the degree that was on the horizon at a given moment, or that represents the position of a planet at a given moment; the point on which an Eclipse or other celestial phenomenon occurred; the places of the Moon's Nodes; or the cusps of the Houses, particularly the First and Tenth. Generally speaking, the term *aspect* is applicable in astrology to any blending of rays that results in their interactivity. The body which has the faster mean motion is said to aspect the slower one.

Aspectarian: A chronological list of all astrological *aspects* (q.v.) formed during a specified period.

Aspirant: A disciple of esoteric philosophy, eligible for initiation.

Asport: The disappearance of a solid object through solid walls or other solid matter; the opposite of *apport* (q.v.).

Astaroth: In demonography, a powerful demon, high-ranking in the infernal empire.

Astika: A Sanskrit term, denoting an individual who acknowledges the authority of the *Veda* (q.v.).

Astikaya: A Sanskrit term for *bodily* or *extended substance*. In Jaina philosophy, only time is unlike a body (*anastikaya*), hence unextended.

Astragalomancy: Foretelling the future by means of dice marked with letters of the alphabet.

Astral body: In occultism, man's ethereal counterpart, a replica of the physical body (the *gross body*), but of a more subtle and tenuous substance, penetrating every nerve, fibre and cell of the physical organism, and constantly in a supersensitive state of vibration and pulsation. It may depart from the gross body for short whiles, but cannot sever its connection with the latter without causing it to die. The more active is the gross body, and the more conscious it is of its physical environment, the more inactive is the astral body. The astral body is most active when the gross body sleeps, and this is when the astral body may communicate with astral bodies of other living persons or of the dead.

Astral light: In occult terminology, the name of a universal living element which is described as an element and a power at the same time and containing the character of all things. It is said to be the storehouse of memory for the Macrocosm, the contents of which may be reimbodied and reincarnated—and at the same time the storehouse of the memory of man's Microcosm, into which he delves to recollect past happenings. While it exists uniformly all throughout the universe its density and activity are increased around certain objects, in particular around the human brain and spinal cord; it is the medium through which thought is transmitted, and its presence around man's nerve cells and conduits enables human beings to perceive impressions on the astral aura and thus to "read by the astral light"—the akashic reading, scientifically called clairvoyance.

Astral plane: In those occult doctrines which believe in various planes of existences beyond the material one (e.g., in Theosophy), the first plane of existence after the death of the physical body. In doctrines which recognize only one plane of existence beyond the material one (e.g., in Rosicrucianism), this term is interpreted as a name for the sphere of non-material existence.

Astral projection: In occult terminology, the partial or complete separation of the astral body (q.v.) from the physical body, and visiting another locality, near or far. This occurs in sleep—though, as a general rule, one does not recall the experience on waking. The adept can command his astral body to go any place he desires in order to make observations and investigations, and acquire essential information.

Astral shell: The personality in its aspect of disintegration after the death of the physical body.

Astral soul: In theosophical terminology, a synonym for the lower manas, the reflection of the higher Ego, and not synonymous with astral body.

Astral sphere: The astral world (q.v.).

Astral world: The first sphere of existence after the death of the body.

Astrological symbols: See: Symbols, astrological.

Astrology: The belief in and study of the influence upon human character of cosmic forces emanating from celestial bodies. There are two fundamentally different methods, or approaches, to astrology: geocentric astrology is based upon calculations of the planetary positions as seen by the observer on the Earth, i.e., using the Earth as a center; heliocentric astrology bases its interpretations upon positions within the solar system with reference to the Sun as the center. As to purpose and application, there are several distinct branches of astrology, such as agricultural, electional, horary, mundane, natal astrology, astrometeorology (q.v.), etc.

Astromancy: A system of divination by means of the stars. (Not synonymous with astrology.)

Astrometeorology: Investigation of the relation between the

Solar system bodies and the weather; the application of the art to the forecasting of weather conditions, earthquakes and severe storms; also known as *meteorological astrology*.

Astronomos: The title given by the priests to the Initiate in the seventh degree of the reception of the mysteries in the Initiation at Thebes in Egypt.

Astrotheology: A system of theology founded on what is known of the heavenly bodies, and of the laws which regulate their movements.

Asura: In Hindu mysticism, a fallen angel or demon, hostile to the gods (*devas*).

Aswattha: The Sanskrit name of the Tree of Knowledge, conceived of as the tree of cosmic life and existence; its roots, extending upward, symbolize the invisible spiritual world, and its branches, spreading downward, symbolize the visible, tangible, material universe.

Ate: In Roman mythology, daughter of Jupiter, goddess of revenge and all evil, inciter of mankind to evil thoughts and deeds.

Atharva Veda: The latest of the four *Vedas* (q.v.), containing many magic charms and incantations, as well as hymns and prayers similar to those in the Rig Veda. (It is often referred to as the "Veda of Occult Powers.")

Atlantean: The fourth *root race* (q.v.) in esoteric philosophy.

Atlantis: The "lost continent" of the fourth *root race* according to esoteric philosophy, said to have lain between Africa and South America.

Atma; atman: Sanskrit for *Spirit*. In occultism, the *Universal Spirit* or *World Soul*.

Atmaswarupa: The Sanskrit term used by Hindu mystic philosophers for the universe. (Literally: *manifestation of the Spirit*.)

Aton: The name (also given as *Aten*) of the Egyptian god personifying the disk of the sun, as the deity of the monotheistic religion which Amenhotep IV, renamed Ikhnaton (or Akhenaten) attempted to introduce in Egypt in the 14th century B.C. This religion did not survive its royal founder and sponsor.

Atonement: A religious act of expressing consciousness of one's sins, as well as penitence and reconciliation.

At-one-ment: A term used in Christian science for the spiritual union with the Immortal Mind.

Atziluth: In Kabbalistic cosmogony, the archetypal world.

Audition: The hearing of voices without the agency of physical auditory senses or organs; the auditory counterpart of *vision* (q.v.), often accompanying the latter.

Augur: A magician-priest of ancient Rome who predicted the future by the flight of birds.

Augury: In ancient Rome, divination by the flight of birds. The word is used generally for all kinds of divination, also for any omen or sign on which divination is or can be based.

Aum: See: *om*.

Aura: In occult terminology, a psychic effluvium that emanates from human and animal bodies and inanimate objects. The aura is multi-colored and brilliant, or dull, according to the character or quality of the person or thing. It is composed of electro-vital and electro-mental magnetism; an envelope surrounding that of which it partakes—visible only to the psychic. To the seer, the aura of a person is an index to his hidden propensities.

Auric egg: In esoteric philosophy, especially in theosophical occultism, the source of the human *aura* (q.v.) and the seat of the higher spiritual and mental faculties.

Austerities: Severe self-discipline of the body, even to self-infliction of cruel torture, for the welfare and purification of the soul or spirit.

Austromancy: Foretelling the future by using the winds as sources of divinatory data.

Automatic drawing: The production of drawing by a medium without control of his conscious self; also, the drawing so produced.

Automatic painting: The production of paintings by a medium without control of his conscious self; also, the painting so produced.

Automatic speech: The phenomenon of a medium's speaking without control of his conscious self.

Automatic writing: The production of script by a medium without control of his conscious self; also, the script so produced.

Automatism: In mediumistic and parapsychological terminology, the collective term for automatic writing, automatic drawing (q.v.), and all other activities performed without the conscious awareness and will of the individual.

Avatar: A Sanskrit term, which in Hindu terminology is used properly in the meaning of "an incarnation of Vishnu." Theosophists and other believers in occultism and esotericism use it in the general meaning of any *divine incarnation*. The word is frequently used also to denote one spiritually highly developed through many incarnations on the material plane of existence. (This is the meaning of the term in Rosicrucianism, in particular.)

Avesta: The sacred book of the Zoroastrians. The original Avesta (also called *Zend*) was said to comprise all knowledge; most of it was destroyed by Alexander. A work of 21 volumes (*nasks*) was prepared out of its remnants in the third century A.D., but only one volume (*Vendidad*) has survived complete.

Avidya: A Sanskrit term for *ignorance*. Unawareness of true reality.

Avyakta: Sanskrit for *unmanifested, undifferentiated;* the uncaused cause of material or phenomenal existence.

Axis mundi: Latin for *axis of the world*. In occult and magical terminology, the point at which communication is made between heaven, earth and hell.

Ayam atma brahma: Sanskrit for *"this self is* brahman." A famous quotation from the Upanishads, alluding to the central theme of the Upanishads—the identity of the human and divine or cosmic.

Azael: In Hebrew mysticism, one of the angels who rebelled against God.

Azazel: The mysterious creature dwelling in the desert to which the Hebrews of biblical times sent forth their *scapegoats* (q.v.). In latter Hebrew mysticism, this name was used as that of one of the fallen angels.

B

Ba: In the ancient Egyptian religion, the soul, which could return to the body so long as the body had not been destroyed.

Baal: The chief male divinity of the Phoenicians, to whom he symbolized the Sun. Baal was worshipped in agricultural festivals as the god of fertility of soil and increaser of flocks. In successive periods of the history of the ancient Semitic races, the name (meaning *Lord*) was assigned to innumerable local deities. (Cf. *Bel.*)

Baalberith: In demonography, a demon, an official of the infernal empire.

Baal-Peor: A Moabite god whose cult included a great many elements of licentiousness and obscenity. It is believed that the name of the demon Belphegor (q.v.) is derived from his name.

Baalzaphon: In demonography, a demon, an official of the infernal empire.

Babylonian: An astrologer; so-called because the Babylonians were famed for their knowledge of astrology.

Bacchic mysteries: See: *Dionysian mysteries.*

Bacchus: The Roman god of wine, identified with the Greek Dionysos.

Bachelor: In demonology and witchcraft, "the name given to his satanic majesty, when he appeared in the guise of a great he-goat, for the purpose of love intercourse with the witches." (L. Spence, *An Encyclopaedia of Occultism.*)

Bad: In Persian mythology, the Jinn ruling winds and storms.

Bael: In demonology, the supreme monarch of the infernal empire.

Balan: In demonography, a king of demons.

Balances: See: *Libra.*

Balder: In the Norse mythology, the son of Odin and Frigga, the god of peace; he was slain by Hoder, acting as an unintentional and unwitting tool of the evil Loki.

Banshee: A nature-spirit believed in Ireland and Scotland to take the form of an old woman, to chant a mournful dirge under the windows of a house in which a person is to die soon.

Baphemetous: The Greek name of the mystic diagram more commonly known as the Pythagorean Pentagon.

Baphomet: In occultism, the Sabbatic goat, in whose form Satan was said to be worshipped at the Witches' Sabbath. (See: *Bachelor.*)

Barau: A Polynesian sorcerer.

Barqu: In demonography, a demon, guardian of the great secret of the *Philosopher's Stone* (q.v.).

Barren signs: The astrological signs Gemini, Leo and Virgo, which are said to signify a tendency toward barrenness.

Barsom: In the rituals of the ancient Parsis, a bunch of twigs cut from the trees amidst appropriate rites and incantations and presented to the temples; only the priests were permitted to carry it during prayers or magical ceremonies.

Bathym: An alternative name of the demon *Marthim.*

B'duh (Beduh, Baduh): In Arabic mythology, a spirit who helps messages to be speedily transmitted to their destinations. His help is ensured by writing the numbers 2-4-6-8 (which represent the letters of the Arabic alphabet, B-D-U-H, spelling his name) as a written invocation.

Bast: See: *Bubastis.*

Bat: In Chinese occult symbology, a symbol of happiness. (Cf. *fu lu shou.*)

Beelzebub: In demonography, the sovereign of the infernal empire.

Behemoth: In demonography, a demon who appears in the form of a huge elephant; often identified with Satan.

Beholding signs: In astrology, those signs which have the same declination, *i.e.*, are at equal distances from the Tropics.

Bel: The Babylonian form of *Baal* (q.v.), a member of the supreme triad of deities: Anu, god of the heavens; Bel, god of the Earth; and Ea, god of the waters.

Belial: Hebrew for *person of baseness* or *wicked person.* The prince of devils, identified with Beelzebub or Satan.

Belisama: Literally, *Queen of Heaven.* The name of a goddess of ancient Gaul.

Beltane: The spring festival celebrated on May Day in the Celtic lands in pre-Christian times.

Benefic: Deemed to have a beneficial influence or effect.

Belomancy: Divination by arrows.

Belphegor: In demonology, the name of a demon, inspirer of discoveries and inventions.

Beltane: The Celtic spring festival, held on May Day.

Beneficent Magic: White Magic (q.v.).

Be-ness: In theosophist terminology, the equivalent of the Sanskrit word *sat* (q.v.).

Benjees: The Devil-worshipping cult of India.

Berith: In demonography, a "Duke of Hell."

Bes: An Egyptian god of pleasure, able to counteract witchcraft.

Berkeleianism: See: *Esse est percipi.*

Bestial signs: In astrology, those signs (q.v.) which have been symbolized by beasts, or animals (Aries, Taurus, Leo, Scorpio, the last half of Sagittarius, Capricorn and Pisces).

Bestiary: Any book which gives illustrations or descriptions of animals, real and mythical.

Bethor: The Olympian Spirit (q.v.) governing Jupiter, ruler of 42 Olympian Provinces of the Universe; his day is Monday.

Bewitchment: An evil spell cast, or an illness caused, by a witch, sorcerer or black magician.

Bezoar: A precious stone said to be found in the innards of animals and to have magical properties.

Bhagavad Gita: Sanskrit for *Song of the Divine One.* The title of a celebrated philosophic epic poem, inserted in the *Mahabharata* (q.v.), containing a dialogue between Krishna and Arjuna, which clearly indicates the relationship between morality and absolute ethical values in the Hindu philosophy of action (*Karma Yoga*); it is considered to be one of the most influential philosophical poems of Sanskrit literature; the exact date of origin is unknown.

Bhagavan: Sanskrit for *God;* the word is used also for a few Sages considered to have achieved absolute one-ness with God.

Bhakta: Sanskrit for *devotee.*

Bhakti: Sanskrit for *devotion.* Worship, faith, religious devotion as a way of spiritual attainment.

Bhakti-marga: Sanskrit for *path of devotion.* The approach to spiritual perfection through loving devotion to God. (See: *Bhakti yoga.*)

Bhakti yoga: The Yoga of love, the quest of union with the Divine Spirit through the *bhakti-marga,* the harmonization of the love nature of man with his prescribed destiny, which is to manifest, in all its purity, the Divine Love of the Creator under its three-fold aspect of life-giver, preserver and upholder. Man is conceived as ultimately reaching the divine union of mystic love by uniting his love nature with that portion of the divine aspect of love and cohesion which is giving him life. The three degrees of Bhakti Yoga are: *Bhaya bhakti, ananaya bhakti,* and *yekanta bhakti* (q.v.).

Bhaya bhakti: In *bhakti yoga* (q.v.), the worship of the deity through formulas, images, rites, etc.

Bhutas: Astral shades of human beings.

Bibliomancy: Divination by means of chapters and verses taken at random in a book.

Bicorporeal signs: See: *Double-bodied signs.*

Bielbog: Literally *white god;* in Slavonic mythology, the power of good opposed to the power of evil (*Czarnobog*).

Bilocation: The phenomenon in which a body occupies or seems to be present in two places simultaneously.

Birraark: A mediumistic magician of certain tribes of Australian aborigines, specializing in communicating with the "ghosts" of the dead.

Birth moment: Astrologers use this term for what they generally regard as the true moment of birth: the moment of the first inspiration of breath after ligation of the umbilical cord, when the infant ceases to receive blood conditioned through the mother's receptivities, and must grow channels of receptivity to cosmic frequencies that accord with those present in the Earth's magnetic field, and through these receptivities it begins to condition its own blood.

Birth rites: The ceremonies practiced by ancient peoples, contemporary primitive tribes, etc., at the birth of a child, to cleanse both the mother and the new-born infant from the impurities of child-birth, to protect the infant from evil spirits and to give him strength and good fortune.

Bitabas: An African (Sudanese) sorcerer.

Black Book, The: A sacred book of the Yezidi (devil worshippers) of Kurdistan.

Black fire: The Kabbalistic term for absolute wisdom, which the finite human mind cannot grasp.

Black magic: The use or abuse of supernormal powers for selfish ends; sorcery, necromancy, the raising of the dead, etc.

Black mass: The mass said in honor of the devil at the Witches' Sabbath.

Black shaman: A shaman (q.v.) who concerns himself exclusively with spirits, demons, and other evil or malignant powers.

Blasting rod: See: *thundering rod.*

Blessing of the New Moon: In the Jewish rituals, an outdoor benediction service on the appearance of the new moon, which marks the beginning of a new month of the Hebrew calendar.

Blood revenge: The duty of a kinsman to kill the killer of his kin; the enforcement of the rule of "a life for a life" in primitive societies.

Boat of the Soul: A vehicle used in funeral rites of Chinese royalty.

Boaz: in Kabalistic and Masonic tradition, the white pillar of bronze cast for Solomon's temple; the symbol of Divine Wisdom (*Hokhmah*, the second of the *Sephiroth*—q.v.).

Bodhisattva: Sanskrit for *existence in wisdom.* In Buddhist terminology, one who has gone through the ten stages (*dasa-bhumi* —q.v.) to spiritual perfection and is qualified to enter Nirvana and become a Buddha, but prefers to remain a Buddha-to-be in order to work for the salvation and deification of all beings.

Bogie; bogy; bogy-man: A demon of malignant disposition and terrifying appearance.

Bogle: A name used in Scotland for an evil spirit.

Bön: A pre-Buddhist, animistic and Shamanistic religion of Tibet.

Book of Changes, The: A Chinese collection of propositions and explanations used in divination, written by various authors of different periods up to the latter part of the third century B.C. (Chinese title: *I Ching*, also known as *Yi King*.)

Book of Splendor: The book *Zohar*, the principal part of the earlier Kabalah (13th century).

Book of the Dead: Any one of a series of ancient Egyptian writings which set forth the substance of the magic, ritual and myths of their respective periods. The "Book" is the total of the inscriptions found on papyrus, tombs, monuments, etc.

Book of the Keys: Title of an ancient Kabalistic work.

Borderline state: With respect to human consciousness and perception, that mental and psychological state in which the objective consciousness blends into the subjective. This state can be self-induced or produced under hypnosis. Many occult authorities maintain that this state is the first stage of man's transition from the material plane of existence to the next one when the physical body dies.

Bosatsu: In Japanese Buddhist terminology, the equivalent of *Bodhisattva* (q.v.).

Botanomancy: Divination by means of plants or herbs.

Boyla: The shamanistic medicine-man of certain tribes of Australian aborigines.

Brahma: In Hindu mythology and occult philosophy, the Creator, as one of the three aspects of *Ishwara*, the Personal God. (Often written *Brahmâ*, to distinguish the word from *Brahma* as an alternative form of *Brahman*—q.v.).

Brahma-loka: In Hinduism, the divine plane of the first emanation, the world of Saguna Brahman (q.v.).

Brahman: In Hinduism and occult philosophy, the Absolute. (Frequently, although incorrectly, referred to also as *Brahma*—q.v.).

Brahmanaspati: (1) A deity in the Rig-Veda. Known in Vedic mythology as Brihaspati, signifying the power of prayer. (2) The Hindu name for the planet Jupiter.

Brahmanic Hinduism: That stage of Hinduism represented in the literature known as the Brahmanas, the period of change from Vedic Hinduism (q.v.) to a thoroughly cosmological, ritualistic and mystic creed, in which priests, sacrifices and magic practices played an important part.

Brahmanism: The predominant form of philosophical, theological, and esoteric speculation of India, sponsored by the Brahman caste which traces its doctrines back to the Vedas (q.v.) and Upanishads (q.v.).

Brahma's Day: In Hindu mythology and occultism, a period of 4,320,000,000 of our years, during which Brahma, having awakened, creates and shapes the material world. At the end of this period, the material world is destroyed by fire and water, Brahma disappears to sleep during the period called *Brahma's Night.*

Brahma's Life: One hundred of *Brahma's Years* (q.v.).

Brahma's Night: In Hindu mythology and occultism, a period of 4,320,000,000 of our years, following *Brahma's Day* (q.v.). Brahma is said to be asleep during his Night, awakens at the end of it, and another *Brahma's Day* commences.

Brahma's Month: Thirty of *Brahma's Days* and *Nights* (q.v.).

Brahma's Year: Three hundred and sixty of *Brahma's Days* and three hundred and sixty of *Brahma's Nights* (q.v.).

Breath of Life: According to the Rosicrucian Manual, "in Rosicrucian teachings this term is used to refer to *Nous.* It is a combination, so to speak, of both the Vital Life Force and Cosmic Consciousness."

Briah: According to the Hebrew Kabalah, the world of creation, produced from the world of Adam Kadmon, the heavenly man. Also called *Briatic World.*

Brother: In esoteric and occult philosophy, an initiate who works toward the accomplishment of his task in all incarnations.

Brother of the left-hand path: An initiate in occultism who works for the forces of evil and opposes the Divine Will, practices black magic, necromancy, etc.

Brother of the shadow: A synonym for *brother of the left-hand path* (q.v.).

Brownie: In the occult lore of Scotland, the name given to dark-featured nocturnal nature-spirits which haunt country and farm houses; believed to be good-natured and bearers of good omen.

Bubastis: Egyptian cat-headed goddess of fire. Also known as Bast.

Buddha: An enlightened and wise individual who has attained perfect wisdom. Specifically applied to Gautama Siddhartha, founder of Buddhism in the sixth century B.C.

Buddhi: A Sanskrit word meaning *Universal Mind.*

Buddhi-Taijasi: Sanskrit for *radiant soul or mind.* In occultism, it means the human soul or mind illuminated by the radiance of the Divine Spirit.

Buddhism: The multifarious forms, philosophic, religious, ethical and sociological, which the teachings of Gautama Buddha have produced, and which form the religion of hundreds of millions in China, Japan, etc. They center around the main doctrine of the *arya satyani,* the four *noble truths* (q.v.), the last of which enables one in eight stages to reach *nirvana* (q.v.): Right views, right resolve, right speech, right conduct, right livelihood, right effort, right mindfulness, right concentration.

Bull: See: *Taurus.*

Bullroarer: An instrument of defensive magic used by the Australian aborigines, also by the Navajo Indians; when whirled, it makes a sound like thunder which is believed to frighten evil spirits.

C

Cabala: See: *Kabalah*.

Cabales; Caballi: In occultism, "the astral bodies of those who died by violence (external or self-inflicted) prior to the end of their natural term of life. These earth-bound, suffering souls are said to wander within the sphere of the attraction of the earth until the end of their natural term of life." (L. W. de Laurence)

Cabinet: The designation of the space, enclosed by curtains, in which mediums claim to condense the psychic energy required for manifestations in the seance room.

Cabiri: A group of minor deities often mentioned in ancient writings as powerful masters of magic. They were probably of Semitic origin, and their worship as gods of mysteries was widespread in Greece, especially in Samothrace, Bœotia and Thessaly.

Cocodemon: A malignant demon, regarded as a fallen angel (q.v.).

Caduceus: The wand of Hermes, or Mercury, the messenger of the gods. A cosmic, magic, or astronomical symbol; its significance changing with its application. Originally a triple-headed serpent, it is now a rod with two serpents twined around it, and two wings at the top. The entwined white and black serpents represent the struggle between good and evil—disease and cure. (Cf. *Aaron's Rod*.)

Caitanya: Sanskrit for *consciousness* or *intelligence;* the universal intelligence or spirit; a quality near the in-it-self aspect of the Absolute Spirit, and hence sometimes a synonym for it.

Calx: In alchemical terminology, a metallic oxide.

Camaxtli: An ancient Mexican war god, often identified with Mixcoatl.

Cambion: The offspring of *incubi* and *succubi* (q.v.).

Camp meeting: The earlier name of the assemblies of spiritualists.

Cancer (The Crab): The fourth sign of the Zodiac. Its symbol (♋), presumably the folded claws of a crab, probably is intended to symbolize the joining together of a male and female spermatozoa—as indicative of the most maternal of all the signs. The Sun is in Cancer annually from June 21 to July 22. Astrologically it is the first thirty-degree arc following the Summer Solstice, marked by the Sun's passing of the Tropic of Cancer, and occupying a position along the Ecliptic from 90° to 120°. It is the "leading" quality of the element Water: negative, cold, moist, phlegmatic, nocturnal, commanding, movable, fruitful, weak, unfortunate, crooked, mute. Ruler, Moon. Exaltation: Jupiter. Detriment: Saturn. Fall: Mars.

Canopic jar: The jar into which the embalmers of ancient Egypt put the intestines and other internal organs of the corpse being embalmed.

Caodaism: An esoteric religion and mystery cult founded in Indo-China in the 1920's, claiming to have received its teaching from the Supreme Being (*Cao Dai*) through spiritualistic implements. It honors Christ, Buddha, Confucius and Lao-Tzu as saviors sent by the same deity. It teaches the existence of the soul, reincarnation and the law of Karma.

Capnomancy: Divination based on the smoke of an altar or a hearth as divinatory sign.

Capricorn (The Goat): The tenth sign of the Zodiac. In Hindu astrology, Makarar—and considered by the ancients to be the most important of all the signs. Its symbol (♑) represents the figure by which the sign is often pictured—that of the forepart of a goat, with the tail of a fish—vaguely suggesting the mermaid. Sometimes also by the sea-goat, or dolphin. It is said to have a reference to the legend of the goat and the Sun gods. The Sun is in Capricorn annually from December 22 to January 20. Astrologically it is the first thirty degrees following the Winter Solstice, marked by the passing of the Sun over the Tropic of Capricorn and occupying a position along the Ecliptic from 270° to 300°. It is the "leading" quality of the element Earth: negative, nocturnal, cold, dry, obeying. Ruler: Saturn. Exaltation: Mars. Detriment: Moon. Fall: Jupiter. Symbolic interpretation: A goat with a fish's tail, signifying extremes of height and depth; changes wrought by time; union of the Christian and Jewish religious dispensations.

Cardinal signs: In astrology, the signs Aries, Cancer, Libra and Capricorn—whose cusps coincide with the cardinal points of the compass: Aries, East; Cancer, North; Libra, West; and Capricorn, South.

Cardinal virtues: The cardinal virtues for a given culture are those which it regards as primary, the others being regarded either as derived from them or as relatively unimportant. Thus the Greeks had four: wisdom, courage, temperance, and justice; to which the Christians added three: faith, hope, and love or charity.

Cartomancy: Divination by cards.

Casting off of sins: The Jewish ceremony, called *Tashlikh* in Hebrew, in which crumbs of bread symbolizing one's sins are thrown into a river, thus symbolizing the casting off of one's sins.

Casting the horoscope: The term used by astrologers to imply the calculations necessary to be made, prior to the delineation of the nativity.

Castle of the Inferior Man: In mysticism, the allegorical name of the seven stages of the soul's ascent toward the Divinity.

Catalepsy: A death-like state of physical coma, bodily rigidity, in which normal functions of the body, including sensations, are suspended and consciousness ceases; it may last from minutes to days. According to certain occultists, it is produced primarily in the astral body during the process of exteriorization.

Cataplexy: Catalepsy (q.v.) in animals.

Catoptromancy: An ancient Greek method of divination by observing images reflected in a mirror suspended in a fountain.

Causal body: "This term denotes the vehicle of the spiritual ego in the higher mind of each individual. It is usually called the immortal soul, for it persists throughout the cycle [of reincarnations]. To it are attached the vehicles of the personality or personal ego, on the lower planes." (G. A. Gaskell)

Causality: The relationship between cause and effect, events, processes, etc.

Cause: Something, the existence of which is a pre-condition of the existence of something else; in the words of Leukippus, "Nothings happens without a ground but everything through a cause and of necessity."

Celestial light: The light which shimmers around certain mystical visions and can be seen only by those who have led a clean life, when the vital spark has almost departed from the physical body.

Celestial voyage: In shamanism, the ecstatic trance of the shaman.

Centaur: In Greek-Roman mythology, a creature who is half man and half horse.

Cerberus: In Greek mythology, the three-headed dog guarding the entrance to Hades, the underworld.

Ceremonial magic: Magic based on the invocation of powers above man's level on the scale of being, and giving man command over elementals (q.v.) by the use of certain rites and rituals.

Ceres: The Roman mother-goddess, identified with the Greek goddess Demeter.

Ceromancy: Divination by interpreting the shapes and positions assumed by melted wax dropped on the floor.

Chain: In spiritualistic terminology, *forming a chain* at a seance means that those sitting around the table join hands, in order to strengthen the magnetic current of their bodies.

Chakra: In Yogi philosophy, one of the stages of the development of spiritual force in man.

Chakra: In theosophical terminology, a sense organ of the ethereal body, visible only to a clairvoyant. There are ten *chakras*, which permit those trained in their use to gain knowledge of the astral world. (Three of the ten *chakras* are used in black magic only.)

Chaldean Oracle: An Oracle venerated as highly by the Chaldeans as was the one at Delphi by the Greeks. It promised victory to anyone who developed masterly will, and taught that "Though Destiny may be written in the stars, it is the mission of the divine soul to raise the human soul above the circle of necessity."

Ch'an school of Buddhism: The Chinese equivalent of the Japanese Zen Buddhism (q.v.).

Ch'ang: Chinese for "Invariables" or universal and eternal laws or principles running through the phenomenal change of the universe. (Lao Tzu.)

Changeling: The little mannikin which, according to Celtic folklore, the "little people" leave in the cradle of a human infant they steal. The changeling, about the size of the infant, has a wizened face and does not grow normally.

Ch'ang sheng: In the philosophy of Lao Tzu, everlasting existence, such as that of Heaven and Earth, because of their "not existing for themselves." In Taoist religious terminology: 1) Long life, as a result of the nourishment of the soul and rich accumulation of virtue. 2) Immortality, to be achieved through internal alchemy and external alchemy (*lien tan*).

Changing Woman: The most beloved deity of the Navajo Indians; mother of Monster Slayer and Child of the Water who slew the monsters which threatened mankind.

Chaomancy: Divination by observing and interpreting atmospheric appearances.

Chaos: The formless, undifferentiated primal matter which existed before Creation, and out of which matter and the universe was formed.

Charm: Any magic word, formula, incantation, object, sign or amulet supposed to possess occult power.

Chasid, Chasidism: See: *Hasid, Hasidism.*

Chat: Sanskrit for *physical body.*

Chela: Sanskrit for *disciple.* (Cf. *accepted chela.*)

Cherub: In Hebrew mysticism, a winged celestial being, part human and part animal, serving as the chariot of the Almighty and as guardian angel. (Plural: *Cherubim.*)

Ch'i: Chinese for *force, spirit.* Used in esoteric terminology also for *breath,* the *vital fluid.* Also as the name of the Spirits of Earth (the gods of the ground and the grain, mountains, rivers and valleys).

Chih jen: Chinese for *the perfect man;* one who has reached a state of mystical union with the universe, or "one who has not separated from the true."

Chin tan: The Chinese term for the alchemical transmutation of mercury into gold.

Ching shen: Chinese for the spirit and soul of man, or "the vital force (*ch'i*) and the keeper of life of man," which is endowed by Heaven as against the physical form which is endowed by Earth.

Chirognomy: That branch of palmistry (q.v.) which purports to deduce a person's intelligence from the form of his hands.

Chiromancy: The art of divination from the shape of the hand and fingers and the lines and other markings which appear on them.

Chirosophy: That branch of palmistry (q.v.) which studies the comparative value of hand forms.

Chit: Sanskrit for *consciousness;* intelligence.

Chiton: Burmese name for evil spirits.

Chrestos: An ancient Greek term, used by Gnostics of the first centuries of Christianity for Christ.

Christ myth: A theory popular in Germany from about 1910. It represents Jesus as either an astral deity who came to earth, suffered, died and rose again, or as the projection of the repressed social, economic and political aspirations of the lower classes in the Roman Empire.

Christian Science: A religion and philosophy, founded in 1875 by Mary Baker Eddy, based on the teaching that God, the Universal Mind, is the only existing reality, man is God's spiritual idea and belongs by right to an order in which there is no sickness, sin, sorrow or death; all such things are errors of man's mortal mind and have no reality for man save as he admits them; if man denies them, they cease to exist.

Christian Spiritualists: Spiritualists who stand by the Bible and emphasize the mastership of Jesus Christ.

Churinga: A fetish of the Australian aborigines: a long piece of wood in which the spirit of one's ancestor is supposed to dwell.

Cihuateteo: In Aztec demonology, evil female demons, the spirits of women who died in childbirth.

Circle: In spiritualist terminology, a group including at least one medium, which holds meetings and seances for the purpose of communicating with the spirits of the dead and other discarnate entities.

Circumambulation: Ceremonial walking around an object or a person. This ritual has been and is used in many religions, mystery ceremonies, etc., and occult philosophy attributes a mystic power and significance to it. It is usually done keeping one's right side toward the object or person encircled, to show respect, to secure protection or good fortune, etc.; walking in the reverse direction shows disrespect and is held to have evil effects.

Civa: See: *Shiva.*

Clairaudience: In occult terminology, the psychic ability to hear sounds or voices regardless of distance.

Clairsentience: An occult term indicating psychic sensitivity; "that peculiar feeling that something is going to happen." Almost everyone possesses instinctive and intuitive clairsentience to some degree, popularly often referred to as a "hunch."

Clairvoyance: In occultism, the ability to see things and events regardless of distance; the gift of spiritual sight ("sight with the inner eye").

Clavicle of Solomon: An alternative designation of the book, *Key of Solomon the King* (q.v.).

Cledonismantia; cledonism: The belief in and divination of the good or evil portent of certain spontaneously spoken words when meeting another person or other persons.

Cleromancy: Divination by studying the shapes formed by pebbles thrown on a flat surface.

Clidomancy: Divination by using a Bible and a hanging key, interpreting the movements of the latter.

Cloud of the Law: See: *Dasa-bhumi.*

Cloven foot: In the lore of Satanism and witchcraft and in demonology, the distinctive mark of the devil.

Cluricane: In Irish folklore, an evil elf who usually appears in the shape of an old man; he is supposed to know where hidden treasure can be found.

Color awareness: According to occult teachings, color and color scheme exercise a tremendous influence on the human mind, and by learning the mastery of colors, man can become the master of his thought power and ruler of his destiny.

Color therapy: The practical application, for therapeutic purposes, of the teaching that color affects emotions, health, mental states and conduct in general. (See: *color awareness*.)

Comasonry: A variety of Freemasonry permitting the initiation of women, too.

Combust: In astrological terminology, a planet is said to be in the combust condition when in extreme closeness to the Sun, the limits variously placed at from 3° to 8°30'.

Commanding signs: The term applied in astrology to the signs Aries, Taurus, Gemini, Cancer, Leo, and Virgo, because they were deemed more powerful by virtue of their nearness to the zenith.

Communicograph: A mechanical instrument for communicating with the spirits of the dead. The *Ashkir-Jobson Communicograph* consists of a small table with a free-swinging pendulum under it, which can make contact with any of a number of small metal plates bearing the letters of the alphabet; when the contact is made, an electric circuit is closed and the proper letter appears, illuminated on the surface of the table. The "spirit messages" are spelled out letter by letter this way.

Community of sensation: In general, the sharing of sensations by persons in psychic or spiritual rapport with each other; also, in hypnotism and trance states.

Compathy: Literally, "with-each-other-feeling." Men feel with each other the same sorrow, the same pain. Only psychical suffering can thus be felt, not physical pain. There is no symagony.

Concentration: The act and state of focusing one's entire attention and perception upon a certain object or idea, to the complete exclusion of all others, and under total inactivity of all the physical senses except the one used in this act (e.g., sight, hearing, etc.).

Conception: According to Ptolemy the sex as well as the incidents relating to a child, prior to its birth, may be deduced from the positions of the planets at the time of conception.

Confucianism: Worship of Confucius, a state cult of China. See: *Ju Chia* and *Ju Chiao*.

Conjunction; conjoined to: Terms used in astrology to indicate the mutual relation of two planets occupying longitudinal positions separated by less than 7°. (Strictly speaking, the conjunction takes place when both occupy exactly the same degree position.)

Conjuration: The method, act or process of summoning supernatural aid by calling on divine or evil forces, by incantation or rituals of sorcery or black magic.

Conjuring lodge: The tent or hut of the North American Indian tribes in which mediumistic practices were held. The primitive form of the seance *cabinet* (q.v.) of modern spiritualists.

Conjuror: A sorcerer or black magician.

Consciousness: A designation applied to conscious mind as opposed to a supposedly unconscious or subconscious mind, and to the whole domain of the physical and non-mental. (See: *Field of consciousness.*)

Contagious magic: Magic based on the belief that things which once have been in contact continue to have an influence on each other after their separation; for instance, that a person can be harmed by the performing of rites of black magic over tufts of his hair, nail parings, discarded personal property, etc.

Contemplation: Knowledge consisting in the partial or complete identification of the knower with the object of knowledge, with the consequent loss of his own personality.

Control: In spiritualism, this term is applied to the state of possession of the medium by an invisible entity which uses the body of the medium as an instrument for communicating with those present at the seance. The term *control* is used also to designate this invisible "operator," also referred to as *guide* (q.v.).

Copper age: The *Dwapara Yuga* (q.v.).

Corpora supercœlestia: This Latin term (meaning *super-heavenly bodies*) is applied by spiritualists to forms regarded as the refined, intelligent elements of astral forms, visible only through highest spiritual perception.

Corybantes: Priests of Cybele who conducted the celebrations of the Phrygian Cybele mysteries.

Cosmecology: This title (meaning *the ecology of the cosmic*) was suggested by Harlan T. Stetson, of the Massachusetts Institute of Technology, for a synthesis of the contemporary sciences of astronomy, electro-physics, geology and biology. He suggested that we trace the correlation between changes of a cosmic origin that affect our terrestrial environment, and periods of optimism and depression in the psychology of the human race.

Cosmic: Relating to or originating from the cosmos.—In Rosicrucian usage, *Cosmic* is used as a noun as well as an adjective. Used as a noun, it means "the Universe as a harmonious relation of all natural and spiritual laws. As used in a Rosicrucian sense, the Divine, Infinite Intelligence of the Supreme Being permeating everything, the creative forces of God" (Rosicrucian Manual). (Cf. *Kosmos, kosmic.*)

Cosmic conditioning: The ancient belief that one's destiny upon earth is ruled by the divine power that placed the stars in the heavens; that every created thing is a result of this influence; and that the Sun is the active principle of good, and the darkness of evil.

Cosmic consciousness: That faculty, as yet possessed only by some exceptionally gifted individuals, but regarded by occultists as the eventual goal of future human evolution, consisting of the conscious awareness of the cosmos, of the life and order of the universe.

Cosmic epochs: According to occult teachings, the constellation in which the sun is astronomically and astrologically, rules the destiny of the world and determines the nature of happenings in our world. The current epoch, which started in 1948, is called Aquarian, and was preceded by the Piscean Epoch (the primitive Christian era), which followed the Aries or Ram Epoch (the Mosaic era), which was preceded by the Taurus Epoch (Egyptian and Hebraic epoch), which followed the Gemini Epoch (the Adamic period).

Cosmic ideation: The theosophist term for "eternal thought impressed on substance or spirit-matter, in the eternity; thought which becomes *active* in the beginning of every new life-cycle." (H. P. Blavatsky)

Cosmic mind: In general, the *Universal Mind* (q.v.); specifically, the mind that is a part of *cosmic consciousness* (q.v.).

Cosmic numbers: In numerology, the oudad (0), the monad (1), the dyad (2), the triad (3), the tetrad (4), the pentad (5), the hexad (6), the heptad (7), the octad (8), the ennead (9), and the decad (10).

Cosmic philosophy: A theory of cosmic evolution originated by

John Fiske and advanced by him as an interpretation of Spencer. (Also called *cosmism.*)

Cosmic picture gallery: The *Akashic Records* (q.v.).

Cosmic psychology: The science of diagnosis whereby the maladjustment of the individual to life can be treated by correctional thinking. It does not concern itself with prediction, fortune-telling, life readings, but deals with reactions developed in the individual by virtue of growth and development during his first day of life, through the law of adaptability to cosmic ray frequencies then present in the Earth's magnetic field, and with experiences resulting from environmental stimulation of a pre-conditioned pattern of emotional reactions.

Cosmical: In astrology, said of the rising or setting of a planet (or a star) when it is near the Sun—hence rises and sets along with it.

Cosmism: See: *Cosmic philosophy.*

Cosmogony: A pictorial treatment of the way in which the world or the universe came into being. In contrast to the most primitive civilizations, the great ethnic stocks of mankind have originated cosmogonies.

Cosmology: A branch of philosophy which treats of the origin and structure of the universe.

Cosmos: The universe, as distinguished from our earth. (Cf. *Kosmos.*)

Councillor gods: A term applied, by the Chaldeans, to the three bright stars in a constellation, which served to mark the position of the ruling planet of that sign, when in the sign.

Countercharm: A charm used to nullify the effect of another charm.

Couril: A web-footed dwarf fairy supposed to haunt Druidic ruins in Ireland and Brittany.

Couvade: The custom, of magic significance, observed by a great many primitive races all over the world, which requires the father of a newborn child to lie in bed for a certain number of days.

Coyote: A cunning and resourceful nature-spirit found in the myths of many American Indian tribes; most tribes regard him as a malignant spirit, but in the myths of some tribes he is a bene-factor of mankind.

Crab: See: *Cancer*.

Crithomancy: An ancient method of divination by observing the pattern formed by grain or particles of flour, in connection with sacrificial rites.

Critical day: In occultism, astrology, etc., a day which is destined or able to bring bad luck.

Cromaat: A mystic word, interpreted as Egyptian for *as in truth*, frequently used as a salutation in the Rosicrucian rituals.

Cross-correspondence: In parapsychological investigations, the term for concordances appearing in *automatic writings* (q.v.), etc., executed by two or more mediums, which are demonstrably not deliberately inserted.

Cross-reference: In spiritualist terminology, the simultaneous delivery of spirit messages through two or more different mediums, with a request to forward them to the right person.

Crow's head: In medieval alchemical terminology, the blackness of the mixture intended to produce the Philosopher's Stone (q.v.).

Crux ansata: A cross consisting of a T shape with an oval loop at the top, used by the ancient Egyptians as the symbol of life.

Cryptesthesia: This expression, literally meaning *hidden sensitivity*, was coined by Professor Richert to serve as a collective term for clairvoyance, clairaudience, psychometry, telepathy, dowsing, premonitions, and in general for perception, of the mechanism of which science is ignorant. The cryptesthesia theory denies and intends to disprove the spiritistic explanations of these phenomena. (Cf. *extrasensory perception*.)

Cryptomnesia: The spontaneous remembering of events or facts of knowledge without being able to recall how or when the event was witnessed or the knowledge acquired.

Crystal-gazing: An ancient method of divination, which induces a state of clairvoyance by gazing into a small crystal globe, in which a picture or series of pictures is seen.

Crystallomancy: *Scrying* (q.v.) using a mirror for the shiny surface gazed at.

Cult: A body of rites and practices associated with the worship or propitiation of a particular divinity or group of supernatural beings.

Culture hero: A historical person whose teachings, doings or accomplishments live on, usually in an idealized version, in the myths, legends and traditions of his tribe, race or people. Culture heroes are usually raised by posterity to a divine or semi-divine status or regarded to have been incarnations of high-ranking gods.

Curse: Any act or word designed to produce harm or injury by supernatural powers; an invocation of supernatural powers to wreak harm or injury upon a person, place or object. A qualified person can destroy the effect of a curse, by a blessing or a counter-curse.

Cusp: (*a*) An astrological term, used to designate the imaginary line which separates a Sign from adjoining Signs, a House from its adjoining Houses; (*b*) an indeterminate but small arc contiguous to the boundary-line between adjacent Signs and Houses, wherein there is uncertainty as to the planet's location at a particular moment, and ambiguity as to the planet's influence in a borderline relationship.

Cybele-Attis mysteries: See: *Phrygian mysteries.*

Cycle: A period of cosmic history, marking the beginning or end of some important event. (Cf. *manvantara.*) In *astrology*, the term is applied primarily to the recurrence of planetary conjunctions.

Cyclops: In ancient Greek-Roman lore, a giant with a single eye, in the middle of his forehead. (Plural: *Cyclopes.*)

Czarnobog: Literally *black god.* In Slavonic mythology, the evil deity, the power of evil fighting the good deity (*Bielbog*).

D

Dactyliomancy; dactilomancy: An ancient form of divination by means of a ring.

Dactyls: Legendary magicians, soothsayers and occult healers, who spread from ancient Phrygia to Italy, Crete and Greece.

Dagda: A god in pre-Christian Irish mythology.

Dakhma: The "tower of silence" where Zoroastrianists leave the bodies of their dead to be devoured by vultures.

Dakshinamurthi: In Hinduism and occult philosophy, a manifestation or aspect of Shiva who "teaches in silence."

Dalai Lama: The temporal head of Lamaism, regarded as the incarnation of the most widely revered *Bodhisattva* (q.v.), Avalokiteshvara.

Danu: In ancient Irish mythology, the goddess of knowledge and culture, daughter of the god Dagda.

Daoine sithe: In Scots Gaelic, *men of peace*, a name for fairies.

Daphnomancy: Divination by interpreting the crackling of a laurel branch thrown into the fire.

Darshan: Sanskrit for *sight*. When a Hindu spiritual leader allows his disciples to enjoy the gift of his presence, he is said to "give them *darshan*." The word is used also in the meaning *philosophical system* or *doctrine*.

Dark Night of the Soul: The final phase in the growth of the New Man, the complete purification of the soul which paves the way to the mystic union with God.

Dasa-bhumi: Sanskrit for *ten stages*. In Buddhist terminology, the ten stages of the spiritual development of a *Bodhisattva* (q.v.) toward Buddhahood. Each school of Buddhism has its own *dasabhumi*, but the most widely accepted set in Mahayana Buddhism

is that set forth in the *Dasa-bhumi Sastra*, viz.: (1) The Stage of
Joy, in which the *Bodhisattva* develops his holy nature and dis-
cards wrong views; (2) the Stage of Purity, in which he attains
the Perfection of Morality; (3) the Stage of Illumination, in
which he attains the Perfection of Patience or Humility, and also
the deepest introspective insight; (4) the Stage of Flaming Wisdom, in which he achieves the Perfection of Meditation and realizes the harmony of the Worldly Truth and the Supreme Truth;
(5) the Stage of Presence, in which he achieves the Perfection of
Wisdom; (7) the Stage of Far-going, in which he attains the Perfection of Expediency by going afar and to save all beings;
(8) the Stage of Immovability, in which he attains the Perfection
of Vow and realizes the principle that all specific characters of
elements (*dharmas*) are unreal; (9) the Stage of Good Wisdom,
in which he achieves the Perfection of Effort, attains the Ten
Holy Powers, and preaches both to the redeemable and the un-
redeemable; (10) the Stage of the Cloud of the Law, in which he
attains mastery of Perfect Knowledge and preaches the Law to
save all creatures, "like the cloud drops rain over all."

Day of Yahweh: In Hebrew mysticism, the Day of Judgment.

Dead man's candles: Luminous phenomena which according to
folklore indicate impending death.

Death coach: The coach in which according to a superstitious
belief found in many countries, Death makes its rounds, calling for
souls to take along.

Debility: An embracive term in astrology, preferably applied to
any planet disadvantageously placed by virtue of its House position; the opposite of *Dignity* (q.v.). Frequently employed loosely
as a synonym of *Detriment* (q.v.).

Decad: In numerology, the number Ten.

Decumbiture: In astrological parlance, an horary figure erected
for the moment when a person is taken ill, to serve as basis for
astrological judgment as to the possible nature, prognosis and
duration of the illness.

Deer: In Chinese occult symbology, a symbol of honor. (Cf.
fu lu shou.)

Defensive magic: The use of magic rituals, incantations, etc.,
for averting or overcoming evil influences.

Deicide: Literally, *god-killing*. The killing of a totem animal or of a priest-kind in primitive religions, either real or symbolic.

Deiknymena: Esoteric knowledge taught or explained by visual demonstration. (The term originates from the Eleusinian mysteries.)

Deism: The belief in one God, creator of the universe, as detached from the world and making no revelations.

Déjà vu: French for *already seen*. The feeling that one has seen somebody or something in the past, even though knowing that he could never have actually. The phenomenon is variously explained by occultists as memory from a previous incarnation, a "memory of the future," etc. The term is extended to apply also to such feelings of familiarity with words or sounds (properly *déjà entendu*, "already heard"), etc.

Decoction: An alchemical term for the practice of dissolving or decomposing a substance by boiling it in a solvent; also, the solution obtained by this process.

Delphic oracle: The famous oracle in ancient Greece, where the seeress Pythia, in a state of trance, answered questions about the future.

Demi-god: In polytheistic religions, the offspring of a god or goddess and a human being. Also, a human being deified after his death.

Demiurge: Greek (*demiurgos*) for *worker for the people*—an old Greek term for *craftsman*. In Platonic philosophy, the term was applied to the Creator of the World, and the Gnostics used it in this sense to designate the inferior deity, creator of the evil world of matter.

Demon: While the term originally meant any superhuman being, benevolent or malevolent, lacking the dignity of a deity, it is customarily used today as meaning an evil entity, hostile to human beings.

Demon of Socrates: The guiding spirit who forewarned the ancient Greek philosopher Socrates of dangers.

Demonocracy: The religion of primitive tribes of devil-worshippers; the belief in the rule by demons and evil spirits.

Demonographer: An author who writes about demons and things connected with them and their doings.

Demonography: The literature of demonology (q.v.).

Demonology: The study of demons and their characteristics, their classification, etc.; a theory of demonic behavior.

Depersonalization: The loss of the sense of personal identity or the sensation of being without material existence.

Dermography: The appearance of writing on the skin of a medium, remaining visible for a few minutes to a few hours.

Dervish: A member of one of the Moslem orders or brotherhoods of mystic ascetics.

Descending arc: In theosophical occultism, the descent of the *monads* (q.v.) from the higher spiritual planes or globes of existence downwards to or toward the physical level of existence. (Also called shadowy arc.)

Determinism: The doctrine that every fact in the universe is guided entirely by law and is dependent upon and conditioned by causes. (Cf. *Karma*.)

Detriment: An astrological term for the placement of a planet in the opposite sign from that of which it is said to be the Ruler; it is frequently applied also to *debility* by sign position, which includes the opposite sign to that in which it is in its exaltation, as well as to those of which it is ruler.

Deva: Sanskrit for *radiant being*. In the Vedic mythology and occult terminology, a celestial being, a god, a malignant supernatural entity or an indifferent supernatural being. The general designation for God in Hinduism. In Zoroastrianism, the name of the evil spirits opposed to Ahura Mazda. In Buddhism, a hero or demigod.

Devachan: A Sanskrit term for the intermediate state between two subsequent incarnations.

Devadatta: Sanskrit for *god-given;* in Yoga, that one of the five vital airs (*vayu*) of the body which performs the function of yawning.

Devanagari: Literally, the *letters of the gods;* the characters of the Sanskrit script.

Devil: The chief of the evil demons. In later Jewish and early Christian usage, he was identified with Satan and regarded as the source of all evil, bent upon enslaving mankind.

Devil worship: The worship, common among primitive or savage tribes and races, of evil demons. Specifically, the worship of Satan or Lucifer.

Dhamma: The Pali version of *dharma* (q.v.).

Dhanamjaya: A Sanskrit term, literally meaning *prize-winner*; in Yoga, that one of the five vital airs (*vayu*) of the outer body which performs the function of hiccuping.

Dharma: Sanskrit for *law*; when used in the metaphysical or esoteric sense, it means those universal laws of Nature that sustain the operation of the Universe and the manifestations of all things; when applied to the individual, it has reference to that code of conduct that sustains the soul, and produces virtue, morality, or religious merit leading toward the development of man.

Dhyana: Sanskrit for *meditation* or the full accord of thinker and thought without interference and without being merged as yet; the seventh of the eight stages of Yoga.

Diakka: A term introduced by A. J. Davis for mischievous spirits communicating with or harassing the living from Summerland (q.v.).

Diana: The Roman goddess of the hunt.

Dichotomy: Literally, *a division into two parts*. In a specific example: the view that man consists of soul and body.

Dignity: In astrological terminology, a condition of placement wherein a planet's influence is strengthened; conditions of placement in which the planet's influence is weakened are termed *debilities*. (Dignities and debilities are of two varieties: essential and accidental.)

Dii adscripticii: The collective name of the minor gods of Roman mythology.

Dingir: An ancient Sumerian word for god or deity, and in general for any superhuman and immortal being.

Dionysian mysteries: The ancient Greek mystery cult, originating in Phrygia, observed at various places by migratory groups of adherents. Originally, the rites were highly orgiastic in character; the devotees imbibed the sacred wine, ate the raw flesh of the sacrificed animal and drank its warm blood, and went into a frenzy of ecstasy, believed to be inspired by the presence of the deity within them. (Cf. *Orphic mysteries*.)

Direct drawing: A mediumistic phenomenon, consisting in the production of a drawing without the direction of the conscious will of the medium, and without the use of his hands. A further development of *automatic drawing* (q.v.).

Direct painting: A mediumistic phenomenon analogous to *direct drawing* (q.v.), but resulting in the production of a painting. A further development of *automatic painting* (q.v.).

Direct voice: A mediumistic term for an isolated voice resounding in space without any visible agency or source. At most seances it issues forth from a trumpet which floats about in the room, serving as a condenser, although it has been heard at many seances without a trumpet, sounding from various parts of the room.

Direct writing: *Automatic writing* (q.v.) produced without any visible physical contact with the medium, and occasionally also without any writing material present.

Discarnate: Existing outside of or without a physical body.

Disciple: A follower or student of a school, doctrine or teacher.

Disembodied: Separated from the body; usually applied to the mind or intelligence.

Dispeller of darkness: The name given by occultists to a teacher or guide toward enlightenment (*guru*).

Dispositor: In astrological terminology, the Ruler of the Sign on the cusp of a House is called the dispositor of a planet posited in that House.

Div: The counterpart in Persian mythology of the devil of medieval Europe.

Divination: The use of occult, esoteric or spiritualistic means, skill or practices for gaining knowledge of the unknown or of the future.

Divine Nothingness: In Jewish mysticism, the principle taught by the Habad school, that "the Divine is without limitation and opposed to all 'something,' which is limited. The divine is the 'nothing' that subsumes all limitation and finiteness." (M. Buber)

Divine Science Church: A religious sect based on the doctrine of divine healing, founded by Melinda E. Cramer in 1885.

Divining rod: A **V**-shaped wooden (hazel) twig or piece of wire, whale bone, etc., 6 to 18 inches in length, used by dowsers to locate underground springs, lodes of metal, or other objects of search. The rod is held rigidly in the hands of the dowser, and a force (called *rhabdic force*) coming from underground, is said to cause it to snap over, revolve or change its shape.

Docta ignorantia: Latin for *learned ignorance;* it refers to men's knowledge of God which unavoidably includes a negative element, since He immeasurably surpasses the knowledge of Him gleaned from this phenomenal world, yet for man this is truly a real learning. Title given to one of his philosophical treatises by Nicholas of Cusa (1401-1464) who understood it in the sense of an insight into the incomprehensibility of the infinite.

Dolmen: A Celtic name given to a structure of two or more upright monoliths supporting a flat roof-stone; dolmens are generally believed to have been tombs, but some authorities assume that they were primitive temples.

Door of the dead: A special opening made in the wall of a house through which to remove a corpse, in order to prevent the ghost of the deceased from finding its way back to plague the survivors. The door of the dead is usually walled up again after the corpse has been removed.

Doppelgänger: The *astral body* (q.v.).

Double: A synonym for *astral body* or *Doppelgänger* (q.v.).

Double-bodied signs: The astrological signs Gemini, Sagittarius and Pisces, so called because their symbols represent two Figures. (Also called *dual* or *bicorporeal signs.*)

Dowser: A sensitive who has the ability to locate underground springs and other objects below the surface of the earth by the use of the *divining rod* (q.v.).

Dowsing: The search for and location of underground springs and other objects under the surface of the earth, by the use of the *divining rod* (q.v.).

Dravya: Sanskrit for *substance,* which is the foundation of the universe and is resolved into nine Eternal Realities, viz. (1) Earth (*Prthivi*), (2) Water (*Apas*), (3) Fire (*Tejas*), (4) Air (*Vayu*), (5) Ether (*Akasha*), (6) Time (*Kala*), (7) Space (*Dik*), (8) Soul (*Atman*), (9) Mind (*Manas*).

Dream body: A term which is more or less a synonym for *astral body* (q.v.).

Dreaming true: The ability to control and have consciousness in one's dreams.

Druids: Priest-magicians of the early Celts.

Druses: A religious sect in Asia Minor, whose faith combines teachings of the Mosaic law, the Christian Gospels, the Koran and the Sufi allegories; they believe in one God, transmigration of the soul, constant spiritual evolution and final perfection.

Dryad: In Greek mythology, a tree-spirit which lives in a tree and dies when the tree is cut down or dies.

Duad: A pair of deities, one good or beneficent, the other evil or malignant.

Dual signs: See: *Doubled-bodied signs.*

Dualism: The doctrine that there exist tw) opposed and mutually antagonistic divine or cosmic forces—one good, the other evil. The belief in a *duad* (q.v.).

Dukhobortsy: Russian for *wrestlers with the spirit.* A Russian religious sect professing mystical doctrines and striving for "spiritual understanding."

Dumb signs: The astrological signs Cancer, Scorpio and Pisces. (Also called *mute signs.*)

Duration: A limited extent of existence in time, more or less long, from a fraction of a second to countless ages.

Dvaita: Sanskrit for *dualism;* that school of Hindu philosophy which denies that the Ultimate Principle (*Brahman*) is the cause of the world, and contends that the soul is a separate principle having an independent existence of its own, and is only associated with the Ultimate Principle.

Dwapara yuga: Sanskrit name of the third age (*yuga*) of a *manvantara;* a fourth less righteous than the preceding one, and lasting 864,000 of our years (two-tenths of the entire *manvantara*).

Dweller: An occult term for malignant or hostile astral doubles of the dead.

Dweller in the body: The Spirit (*purusha*—q.v.).

Dweller on the Threshold: In occult terminology, a demon or evil elemental or nature-spirit capable of *obsession* (q.v.). The term was coined by Bulwer Lytton.

Dyad: In numerology, the number Two.

Dyaus: The ancient Aryan god of the sky.

Dynamistograph: A complicated mechanical instrument built, allegedly under spirit guidance, by two Dutch physicians for establishing direct communication with the spirit world without using a medium.

Dysteleology: The term for the forbidding and frustrating aspects of life (such as unfavorable environmental factors, organic maladaptations, the struggle for existence, disease, death, etc.) which make difficult, if not impossible, the theory that there are good purposes predominantly at work in the world.

Dzyan: The Tibetan equivalent of the Buddhist term *dhyana* (q.v.).

E

Ea: In Babylonian and Assyrian mythology, the god of waters and of wisdom, crafts and learning, especially of the magical arts; the third member of the Babylonian triad of gods (Anu, Enlil, Ea).

Earth signs: In astrology, this term is applied to the signs of the Earth Triplicity: Taurus, Virgo, Capricorn. The ancients symbolized these types by the Earth element, because of their predominant "Earthiness" or practicality.

Eating the god: See: *Sacramental meal; theophagy.*

Ecstasis: See: *Ecstasy.*

Ecstasy: A state of rapture in which visions of the invisible world unfold; a shift of human perception from the material world to the spiritual realm. Usually said to be concomitant with a spiritual union with higher reality.

Ectenic force: *Psychic force* (q.v.).

Ectoplasm: A term coined by Professor Richet (a contraction of the Greek words *ektos*, exteriorized, and *plasma*, substance) for the mysterious protoplasmic substance which streams forth from the bodies of mediums, producing super-physical phenomena, including materializations, under manipulation by a discarnate intelligence. Ectoplasm is described as matter which is invisible and impalpable in its primary state, but assuming the state of a vapor, liquid or solid, according to its stage of condensation. It emits an ozone-like smell. The ectoplasm is considered by spiritualists to be the materialization of the astral body.

Eddas: The heroic literature of the old Norse, written in Old

Icelandic (12th-13th centuries A.D.); our chief source of knowledge of Norse mythology.

Effluvium theory; efflux theory: A theory of early Greek thinkers that perception is mediated by *effluvia* or *simulacra* projected by physical objects and impinging upon the organs of sense. Thus Empedocles developed the theory of effluxes in conjunction with the principle that "like perceives only like" (*similia similibus percipiuntur*), that an element in the external world can only be perceived by the *same* element in the body.

Efreet: See: *Afreet.*

Ego: The consciousness of being oneself. According to the teachings of esoteric philosophy, two Egos co-exist in man: the mortal, personal Ego which it calls *personality*, and the divine, impersonal Ego which it designates as *individuality*.

Egoity: In occult terminology, a synonym of *individuality* (q.v.).

Eidolism: The body of the belief about disembodied entities, ghosts, etc.

Eidolon: Greek name for the *astral body* or *Kama Rupa* (q.v.).

Eileithya: A goddess of prehistoric Crete (mentioned by Homer); one of her cave temples was discovered at Amnisos (Candia).

Ekam adwaitam: Sanskrit for *the One without a second;* the famous definition of God in the Chandogya Upanishad.

Elder brother: A member of the Great White Lodge (q.v.), a high initiate in occultism and esoteric sciences whose efforts and diligence have made him attain a higher degree of spiritual evolution than the ordinary student of occultism. Referred to in occult literature also as Adept, Great Initiate, Master, Master Occultist, Master of Wisdom, or Rishi.

Election of days: In occultism, especially in astrology, the determination of the day or days on which a certain act can be most advantageously performed. (Cf. *electional astrology.*)

Electional astrology: An astrological method, the aim of which is to permit the choice of a suitable time for commencing any honestly conceived and reasonable project or endeavor, such as a marriage, journey, law-suit, building operation, engaging in a new business or profession, the reconciling of opponents, drawing up a will, buying land or house, planting a garden, launching a ship, or moving into a new home.

Element: According to occult philosophy, the four elements of the material world are Air, Earth, Fire and Water (symbolizing, respectively, the gaseous, solid and liquid states and heat or energy).

Elemental: A spirit evolved in and from, and inhabiting, one of the four elements—a *sylph* (spirit of the air), a *gnome* (spirit of the earth), a *salamander* (spirit of the fire), or an *undine* (spirit of the water). Occultists regard elementals as beings having substance, but visible only to those who have inner sight; some elementals are regarded benign, others as malignant. (Cf. *elemental essence.*)

Elemental essence: According to occultism, a substance existing on the subtler planes (q.v.), which concentrated thought or desire can mold into entities called *elementals* (q.v.).

Elementaries: In occult terminology, the astral corpses of the dead. An Elementary is the ethereal counterpart of the person no longer alive; as the physical body is dissolved into the elements to which it belongs, also the Elementary is decomposed into its astral elements. Elementaries of good persons decompose soon, while those of the wicked may exist for a long time. Theosophy uses the word Elementary in the meaning of "the disembodied souls of the depraved."

Elementary spirit: An elemental (q.v.).

Eleusinian mysteries: The oldest of all Greek mysteries, known to have been performed as early as the 19th century B.C. They were held in the vicinity of Eleusia, near Athens. They honored the mother-goddess Demeter and her daughter Persephone who was abducted by Hades into the underworld and later was restored to Demeter by Zeus for eight months in each year. Thus, the rites seem to have originated as agrarian ceremonies to insure divine help for the fertility and productivity of the soil, Demeter symbolizing the earth and Persephone the seed. Later, the rites took on an occult significance, were ascribed the power to insure happiness in the world after death, and the power to give the initiate true enlightenment and understanding in this life and on the next plane of existence.

Elf: A wandering nature-spirit appearing in unfrequented places; elves are believed to appear in tiny human forms, and generally to be mischievous, often benevolent and helpful.

Elf-fire: *Ignis fatuus* (q.v.).

Elfin: Elf-like, fairy-like; relating or pertaining to elves.

Elixir of life: The substance sought by the alchemists, as one that can extend life indefinitely and transmute base metals into gold.

Elohim: A Semitic word for *gods;* in Judaism, the name used instead of the ineffable name, Yahveh or Jehovah, of the One God.

Elongation: A mediumistic phenomenon, observed at several seances, consisting in a lengthening of the body of the medium, attributed by the spiritualists to the action of spirits of the dead.

Elysian Fields; Elysium: In classical mythology, the place in the underworld which was the abode of the souls of the righteous after their death.

Emanation: The psychic force or effluence, often described also as a radiation or vibration of magnetic force, said to issue forth from all physical bodies and objects and surround them like a halo or aura.

Emanation doctrine: The occultist doctrine of emanation teaches that nothing can be evolved without first being involved —meaning that evolution as a way of embryonic development and eventual birth of the individual is secondary to spiritual power, the guidance by intelligent forces.

Emma-O: In Japanese Buddhism, the god who is the ruler of the underworld and judges the dead.

Emotional body: A synonym used by many occult authors for the *astral body* (q.v.).

Empathy: The projection by the mind into an object of the subjective feeling of bodily posture and attitude which result from the tendency of the body to conform to the spatial organization of the object (e.g., the tendency to imitate the outstretched hands of a statue).

Empirical: Based on observation, experience or experiment.

En-Soph: The Limitless Deity of early Hebrew metaphysicists, interpreted as the "Supreme God" of the modern Kabalists.

Enchiridion: A collection of magical prescriptions and incantations for protection against illness and misfortune, dating from the ninth century A.D.

Enki: The Sumerian god of the earth, sweet waters, wisdom and profundity of mind. He was sometimes identified with Ea.

Enlil: The Sumerian and Babylonian god of wind and storm, second of the Babylonian triad of gods (the other two were Anu and Ea).

Ennead: In numerology, the number Nine.

Entered apprentice: In Freemasonry, one who has been given the first degree of initiation.

Ephemeris (plural: *ephemerides*). An almanac listing the ephemeral or rapidly changing position which each of the bodies of the solar system will occupy on each day of the year: their longitude, latitude, declination, and similar astronomical phenomena. A set of ephemerides which includes the year of the native's birth, is essential in the erection of a horoscope. The astronomer's ephemeris lists these positions in heliocentric terms; that of the astrologer, in geocentric terms.

Epiphenomenalism: A materialistic theory, which holds that consciousness is, in relation to the neural processes which underlie it, a mere *epiphenomenon* (q.v.).

Epiphenomenon: A by-product of a basic process which exerts no appreciable influence on the subsequent development of the process.

Epistemology: That branch of philosophy which investigates the origin, structure, methods and validity of knowledge.

Epopteia: The advanced degree of initiation in the Eleusinian mysteries.

Erh: A Chinese term designating the active or male principle (*yang*) and the passive or female principle (*yin*), which are the products of Tao and which produce the myriad of things.

Erodinium: A vision or symbolic dream; a pictorial or allegorical representation of some future event.

Eros: In Platonism, the driving force of life aspiring to the absolute Good.

Eschatology: That part of systematic or dogmatic theology dealing with the last things, namely, death, judgment, heaven and hell, and also with the end of the world. Also applied by philosophers to the complexus of theories relating to the ultimate end of mankind and the final stages of the physical cosmos.

Esoteric: Secret, not accessible to the uninitiated. When such information is published it ceases to be esoteric and becomes *exoteric*, which means that the facts have become the property of the rest of humanity.

Esoteric Buddhism: The mystic or occultistic schools of Buddhism. Specifically, Lamaism (q.v.).

Esoteric language: Any artificial *mystery language* (q.v.) invented and used by initiates for the safeguarding of their secrets.

Esoteric Sciences: The *Occult Sciences* (q.v.).

Esotericism: The secret or occult doctrines or sciences; belief in or practice of such doctrines or sciences.

Esoterism: Occult or esoteric character or property. Also, a synonym for *esoteric science.*

ESP: *Extrasensory perception* (q.v.).

Esse est percipi: Latin for *to be is to be perceived.* The maxim formulated by Bishop George Berkeley (1685-1753) expressing that a material world of bodies does not exist except in perceptibility—that things cannot exist unless perceived by some mind, and therefore only mind (divine mind) and mental content (ideas) exist.

Essence: That by which a thing is what it is, as distinguished from the thing's existence, properties or attributes.

Eternity: An infinite extent of time, in which every event is future at one time, present at another, past at another. (Cf. *future.*)

Ether: The substance which, according to occultism, fills all space and pervades all matter.

Etheric double: In occult terminology, the invisible vehicle of the soul, the manifestation of physical vitality; it is constant and does not change throughout the cycles of life and death, but it is not eternal, for it is eventually re-absorbed into the elements of which it is composed. It is considered the invisible part of the physical body, extending slightly beyond the latter and able to combine with other subtle substance. Also called *vital body* or, in Sanskrit, *lingasharira.*

Etheric vision: In theosophical terminology, the power of vision of the etheric double (q.v.).

Ethics: That study or discipline which concerns itself with judgments of approval and disapproval, judgments as to the rightness or wrongness, goodness or badness, virtue or vice, desirability or wisdom of actions, dispositions, ends, objects, or states of affairs.

ETP: See: *Extratemporal perception.*

Etz Hayim: Hebrew for *Tree of Life.* The title of a book by Hayim Vital Calabrese, disciple of Isaak Luria, explaining the Kabalistic system of the latter.

Eudœmonism: The Theory, first proposed in Western philosophy by Aristotle, that the aim of the good life is happiness or well-being.

Eurhythmy; eurythmy: An art devised by Rudolf Steiner, the founder of anthroposophy (q.v.), to "translate into movement the rhythm which permeates man and Nature" and to manifest visibly the "inner essence of speech and tone."

Evil eye: The power of fascination (q.v.) or of harming others by a look.

Evil spirit: According to spiritualistic philosophy, the spirit of a bad man inhabiting the lower spheres from which it can reach a medium, and may even oust the *control* (q.v.) of an unwilling medium.

Evocation: The art or act of summoning *elementals* (q.v.) or other discarnate entities.

Evolution: A continuous process of orderly change and development toward a higher or more complex state.

Evolutionism: The view that the universe and life in all of their manifestations and nature in all of its aspects are the product of development.

Exorcise: To cast out an evil spirit.

Exorcism: The expulsion of malevolent spirits or demons from possessed persons, objects or places, by the utterance of an incantation or formula seeking the aid of a more powerful spirit or deity, usually invoked by name. The term is often applied also to any act or ritual, whether or not including the speaking of a formula, by which malevolent spirits are expelled.

Exoteric: Exposed, visible. Antithesis of *esoteric* (q.v.).

Externalization: The mental act by which sensory data originally considered to be internal are projected into the external world.

Externalize: In astrological parlance, said of the event which transpires when an astrological influence is incited to action by contact with a circumstance of environment. The thought is based upon the theory that astrological influences have to do with the mental and emotional conditioning that determines the nature of the individual's reaction to circumstances, but that they do not of themselves produce events.

Extra-cosmic: Outside of the cosmos. According to esoteric philosophy, nothing can be extra-cosmic, because the cosmos (Nature) is infinite and includes everything, and nothing can be outside of it.

Extra-retinal vision: The faculty, claimed by many occultists and spiritualists to be attainable, of using the skin for seeing, instead of the eyes. It is claimed that this actually constitutes sight with the *etheric body*.

Extrasensory perception (ESP): A term coined by Dr. J. B. Rhine of Duke University; defined as "response to an external event not presented to any known sense" (*The Journal of Parapsychology*).

Extratemporal perception (ETP): A newly coined and not as yet generally accepted term for extrasensory perception through time as well as distance in space; the ability to see into the past and the future.

Exuvial magic: A form of contagious magic (q.v.) in which severed parts of the body of an intended victim (nail parings, strands of hair, etc.) are used by a black magician.

Eyeless sight: See: *Extra-retinal vision*.

F

Faculty: Medieval psychology distinguishes several faculties of the soul which are said to be really distinct from each other and from the substance of the soul. According to Aquinas the distinction is based on objects and operations. The faculties are conceived as accidents of the soul's substance, but as pertaining essentially to its nature, therefore "proper accidents." The soul operates by means of the faculties.

Faculty psychology: The conception of mind as the unity in a number of special faculties, like sensibility, intelligence, volition, by reference to which individual processes of sensation, thought or will are explained. Faculty psychology, which originated in Plato's division of the soul into the appetitive, the spirited and the rational faculties, was the dominant psychology of the Middle Ages. It is usually associated with the Soul Substance Theory of Mind.

Fairy: A supernatural being, usually regarded as benign but inclined to mischief.

Faith: According to St. Augustine, faith means, to believe that which one does not see. (*Fides ergo est, quod non vides credere.*) That is the reason why faith is praiseworthy.

Faith healing: A cure effected by the belief that disease and pain can be counteracted and cast out by faith in the Divine Power.

Fakir: The term, properly, designates a Moslem mendicant ascetic and miracle-worker of India. It is often, incorrectly, applied to Hindu ascetics, too. According to Yogi Ramacharaka (in *The Philosophies and Religions of India*), "the secret of the fakir's power generally consists in his ability to produce a mental illusion, or *Maya*, whereby the senses of the bystanders are deluded and the people made to appear to witness things that have no basis in fact. Another class of effects is produced by the control of *Prana* (or Vital Force) by the concentrated Will of the performer, so that heavy objects are moved around in defiance of the law of gravitation, and even the human body at times being floated about in the air . . ."

Fallen angel: An angel cast out from heaven for his sins, or for rebelling against God, and become an evil demon.

Familiar: A spirit who accompanies, and often helps, a magician, sorcerer or witch.

Familiarity: In astrology, a term used by Ptolemy to indicate an aspect or parallel between two bodies; or their mutual disposition, as when each is in the other's Sign or House.

Fana: In Sufism, the "self-attenuation," or "self-effacement," the final stage on the way to mystic union with God (*tariqat*), the cleansing of the mirror of one's impersonal heart and the unfettering from the attachment to material limitations which prevent the soul from apprehending the splendor of the "Real" which is behind and within all appearances. Four degrees of *fana* are described by the Sufi mystics: the *fana fi seheikh*, the complete suppression of one's personality in obedience to one's superior; the *fana fir Rasul*, self-attenuation or effacement of one's personality in the gratitude for the Prophet, the vehicle of the grace of God; *fana Fillah*, self-effacement or self-attenuation in God; and *fana al fana*, the attenuation of the attenuation, the stage beyond consciousness and unconsciousness.

Fanaticism: Zeal so excessive and irrational as to impair self-criticism and destroy moral perspective.

Fang shih: Chinese for *man with formulae*. A primitive Chinese priest-magician.

Fang shui: A Chinese term for magic and occult arts.

Far-going, Stage of: See: *Dasa-bhumi*.

Fascination: In the terminology of occultism, magic and witchcraft, this word means a charm, bewitchment, enchantment.

Fat of the sorcerers: The human fat which sorcerers and witches were accused, in the Middle Ages, of using.

Fatalism: The belief that all events and human activities are predetermined by divine power.

Fates: The three Roman goddesses (*Parcæ*) who presided over the birth and life of mankind. Their names were Atropos, Clotho and Lachesis.

Father-Mother: In esoteric philosophy, the world substance or world soul (q.v.). In Christian Science, a name for God.

Faun: A nature spirit, half man, half goat, venerated as a rural deity by the ancient Romans. The Fauns were attendants of Pan.

Fay: Fairy.

Felicific: Conducive to pleasure or happiness.

Fellow of the Craft: In Freemasonry, an individual who has attained the second degree of initiation.

Feminine principle; female force: In esoteric philosophy, the passive, negative or receptive aspect of the cosmic order, force or of the deity. Matter, wisdom, form are usually conceived of as feminine and are represented by goddesses in the pantheons of the polytheistic religions.

Fenrir: In Norse mythology, a wolfish monster, offspring of Loki. One of the enemies of the Norse gods, he is to swallow Odin himself at the last day, and also to swallow the sun. (Also called *Fenrisulf.*)

Fetch: The name given in Ireland to a *wraith* (q.v.).

Fetch-lights: Mysterious luminous apparitions which the folk-lore interprets as indications of impending death.

Fetish: A material object venerated as the temporary or permanent abode of a soul or spirit.

Fetishism: The belief in fetishes or the worship of a fetish as a deity.

Field of consciousness: The sum total of items embraced within an individual's consciousness at any given moment. The total field consists of: (a) the *focus*, where the concentration of attention is maximal, and (b) a *margin, periphery* or *fringe* of a diminishing degree of attention which gradually fades to zero.

Figure: An astrological or Celestial Figure, variously called Geniture, Map, Scheme, Chart, Theme, Mirror of Heaven, Nativity or Horoscope, as cast, erected or drawn by modern astrologers, consists of a circle of the heavens, representing the 360° of the Earth's orbit, divided into twelve arcs—resembling a wheel of twelve spokes. These arcs may represent Signs of 30° each beginning at the Spring equinoctial point, or Houses of an indeterminate number of degrees beginning at an ascending degree. A Solar Figure, used where a specific moment of birth is not known, employs the Sun's degree as the point of beginning, or Ascendant. The Houses or geo-arcs, based upon the degree rising in the east at the specific moment for which the Figure is cast, supposedly represent the number of degrees which pass over the horizon in two hours from that particular longitude and latitude and on that day. The Sign-divisions, or heliarcs, are thus subdivisions of the Earth's annual orbit round the Sun, while the House-divisions, or geo-arcs, are subdivisions of the daily orbit of a particular point on the Earth's surface around the Earth's axis.

Figurine: A small carved or molded figure of a human being, animal, bird, etc.

Finalism: The belief that the universe is striving for definite ends or for one supreme end.

Finite god: A god whose power is limited by realities which are not his own creation.

Fire: Esoterically, one of the four Elements. In the teachings of Rosicrucians and Hermetists, fire, like man, has a body (the visible flame), a soul (astral fire) and spirit, and it has a fourfold aspect—heat (equivalent to life), light (equivalent to mind), electricity (molecular powers), and the radical cause of its existence.

Fire Philosophers: A designation applied to the medieval alchemists and Hermetists and also to the Rosicrucians.

Fire signs: In astrology, the "inspirational" signs: Aries, Leo, Sagittarius.

Fire-worship, fire-worshipper: An expression often used to refer to Zoroastrianism (q.v.) and its adherents.

First heaven: The outermost sphere of the Aristotelian cosmology, the sphere of the fixed stars.

First fruits: The offering of the first produce of the earth, the first animals killed or trapped in the hunting season, the firstlings of the flock, etc., to the gods most concerned with that particular activity which produced these first fruits, etc., or to the priests of those gods. In ancient days, the practice extended sometimes also to the first child of a man.

Fishes: See: *Pisces.*

Five Agents: See: *Wu hsing.*

Flagae: Familiar spirits; spirits visible in mirrors and able to reveal certain things.

Flaming Wisdom, Stage of: See: *Dasa-bhumi.*

Flexed: An alternate astrological term, preferred by some modern astrologers, for the *mutable signs.*

Fluid body: A synonymous term for *astral body* (q.v.).

Flux: The characteristic of time, by virtue of which all things change inevitably.

Fohat: A Tibetan term for the primordial cosmic substance of occult teachings.

Folklore: The surviving beliefs, legends, myths and traditions of a people, usually transmitted by word of mouth.

Foolish fire: *Ignis fatuus* (q.v.).

Forcas (Foras, Furcas): In demonography, a powerful demon of the infernal empire.

Foreknowledge: Knowledge of the future.

Forest Books: See: *Aranyakas.*

Formalism: The attachment of great significance to the scrupulous observance of external rules.

Fortified: An astrological term, meaning strongly placed (either elevated, in a congenial Sign, or well-aspected).

Fortuna: The Roman goddess of fortune, one of the most powerful goddesses of the Roman pantheon; she was believed to bestow riches or poverty on mortals.

Fortune-telling: Divination; foretelling the future.

Fortunes: In astrological terminology, the benefic planets: Jupiter, the "Greater Fortune"; and Venus, the "Lesser Fortune." The Sun and Mercury, or by some authorities the Moon and Mercury, when well placed and aspected, particularly if by Jupiter or Venus, are sometimes so classed.

Four-footed signs: See: *Quadrupedal signs.*

Four Noble Truths: The *Aryani Satyani,* the four basic principles of the teachings of Gautama Buddha: the Truth of Suffering, the Truth of the Cause of Suffering, the Truth of the Cessation of Suffering, the Truth of the Path to the Ending of Suffering.

Fourth dimension: A higher order of space, additional to the three known dimensions of height, width and length; a direction which is neither up-or-down nor right-or-left nor back-or-forth, but at right angles to all three. Many philosophers consider *time* (duration, the past-or-present direction) a fourth dimension—but the "fourth dimension" just described is conceived of as a fourth *spatial* dimension. In occult terminology, the fourth dimension has to do with internal qualities which, when seen in the astral light, become visible. It has been defined as "the sum of the other three dimensions," and also as "man's expanding sense of time."

Fravashi: In Zoroastrian occultism, the guardian angel of the believer.

Freemasonry: A world-wide philosophical fraternal institution. Its origins are lost in the immemorial past, although it is claimed to have been founded at the time of the building of Solomon's Temple; its present organization dates from 1717, the establishment of the premier Grand Lodge of England. It teaches morality and basic religion by means of symbols, particularly those derived from the builder's craft; its basic doctrines include belief in God, the Great Architect of the Universe, and belief in the immortality of the soul. A great deal of ancient and medieval occult lore, particularly of the Kabalah and of alchemy, has been retained by the Order in a more or less modified form. According to H. L. Haywood, in *Supplement to Mackey's Encyclopedia of Freemasonry* (copyright, 1946, by the Masonic History Company), Vol. III, p. 1234, "A Masonic Lodge represents a body of workmen in which each member has a station or place corresponding to his task or function." It is stated in the same volume (p. 1485) that "there is no occultism in Freemasonry, though the word is often used loosely in the Ritual, as a synonym for 'arcane.' The correct Masonic word is 'esoteric.' "

Free-will: A doctrine that applies to the exercise of the will in overcoming the obstacles of terrestrial environment and cosmic influences, whereby so to control and direct cosmic forces operating at a given time, as to transmute them into power under control. It is opposed to any such yielding to an influence as that which is called Fate.

Fruitful signs: In astrology, Cancer, Scorpio and Pisces; the Water Signs.

Frigga: Wife of Odin in Norse mythology, mother of Thor, Balder and other gods, patroness of conjugal love. Variously regarded as goddess of the earth and air.

Frustration: A term used in horary astrology when one planet is applying to an aspect of another, which aspect would tend to signify some event; but before such aspect culminates, a third planet, by its swifter motion, interposes to anticipate the culmination of the forming aspect by completing one of its own.

Fu: A Chinese term, meaning correspondence, especially that between man and the universe in the macrocosm-microcosm relationship.

Fu lu shou: In Chinese philosophy, the *Three Plenties*—blessing or happiness, official emolument and the honor which it brings, and longevity. They are also called the Three Stars, as each of them is believed to be dependent on a star-god. They are represented either by the three corresponding Chinese ideographic characters, or by a bat (*fu*) symbolizing happiness, a deer (*lu*) symbolizing honor, and a peach (*shou*) symbolizing longevity, or by a smiling figure, with or without children surrounding him, to represent happiness, an official to represent honor, and an old man to represent longevity. These representations are used as charms, as objects of worship, or simply as felicitations.

Funke: German for *spark*. In the philosophy of J. G. Fichte, the divine spark, the life that stirs and wells up within the individual.

Furies: In Roman mythology, the three sisters Alecto, Megæra and Tisiphone, punishers of evildoers, personifications of rage, envy and slaughter.

Future: That part of time which includes all the events which will happen. According to many occultists and esoteric philosophers, the future co-exists with the present and the past, time is indivisible, unchangeable, and past, present and future are merely concepts of the human mind which moves along a "time track" through the reality which is time; foreknowledge, prophecy, etc., can be explained as glimpses ahead along the time track.

G

Gabars: The popular name for the Zoroastrians living in Persia. (Also called *Ghebers*.)

Galvanic mirror: A concave copper disk and a convex zinc disk joined together and magnetized; used for *scrying* (q.v.).

Gameway ceremonials: Magic hunting rites of the Navajo Indians.

Gamut: See: *Notes of the gamut*.

Gandharvas: In Vedic lore, the divine musicians in Indra's heaven; they possess mysterious power over women.

Ganesha: The elephant-headed divinity of Shivaism. Ganesha, son of Shiva, is the god of good luck, prosperity and wisdom, and the remover of obstacles.

Ganga: Sudanese magic.

Garbha: Sanskrit for *seed*. The creative power that lies at the bottom of the world, hypostatized in or symbolized by the germ or seed. In cosmologico-metaphysical conception it is allied to such *termini technici* as *hiranyagarbha* (golden germ), *bija* (seed), *retas* (semen), *yoni* (womb), *anda* (egg, world-egg), *jan* (to give birth to), *srj* (to pour out), etc., descriptive of psycho-cosmogony from the earliest days of Indian philosophy.

Gastromancy: Divination by gazing into a vessel filled with water, or divination by ventriloquist sounds.

Gates of reason: According to a Hebrew mystic legend, there are fifty gates to reason, of which forty-nine were disclosed to Moses.

Gathas: The oldest part of the Avesta, containing the most authentic version of the teachings of Zoroaster.

Gehenna: The word is derived from the Hebrew *Ge Hinnom*, the Valley of Hinnom, near Jerusalem, where the ancient Israelites sacrificed children to the god Moloch; in later times, the valley was regarded as a place of refuse, where fires were kept continually burning to prevent pestilence. The name *Gehenna* was adopted for the "bottomless pit" of eternal fire where the wicked are thrust after death and punished and tormented forever.

Geloscopy: Divination by observing a person's manner of laughing.

Gelug: The reformed sect of Lamaism (Tibetan Buddhism); called the Yellow Sect. Its head and representative, the Dalai Lama, has temporal rule over Tibet.

Gemarah: Hebrew for *completion;* the name of the larger and latter part of the *Talmud* (q.v.) discussing the *Mishnah* (q.v.) and incorporating also vast materials not closely related to the Mishnah topics. The 1812 authorities of the Gemarah are known as *Amoraim* (speakers). Its contents bears on *Halaeha* (law) and *Aggadah* (tale), i.e., non-legal material like legends, history, science, ethics, philosophy, biography, etc. There are two Gemarahs better known as Talmuds: the Jerusalem (i.e., Palestinian) Talmud and the Babylonian Talmud.

Gemini (The Twins): The third sign of the Zodiac. Its symbol (♊) represents two pieces of wood bound together, symbolical of the unremitting conflict of contradictory mental processes. The Sun is in Gemini annually from May 21 to June 20. Astrologically it is the thirty degree arc immediately preceding the Summer Solstice, marked by the passing of the Sun over the Tropic of Cancer, and occupying a position along the Ecliptic from 60° to 90°. It is the "mutable" quality of the element Air: positive, dual. Ruler: Mercury. Detriment: Jupiter. Symbolic interpretation: Castor and Pollux; Bohas and Jakin, of Solomon's Temple; the Pillars of Hercules.

Gemini era: See: *Cosmic epochs.*

Genethliacal astrology: Natal astrology—which deals with the geniture in a nativity (q.v.).

Genethlialogy: That department of astrology which deals with the birth of individuals, so as to form a judgment of the characteristics of a person from a map of the heavens cast for his given birth moment.

Genie: See: *Jinn.*

Geniture: An astrological term, approximately synonymous with Nativity, as referring to the subject whose birth horoscope is under consideration. (A reasonable discrimination would be to use the term Nativity in reference to the person, and the term Geniture in reference to the configurations which show in his birth map.)

Genius: In occult terminology, a nature-spirit; the personification of the indwelling dynamic force which activates an object or phenomenon, gives it energy and determines its effectual and organic existence. Also, a spirit, especially in classical literature, which accompanies a person throughout his entire earthly life as a protective (beneficent genius) or destructive (evil genius) force. (Plural: *genii.*) The word is frequently, but improperly, used also as a synonym for *Jinn* (q.v.).

Geomancy: Divination by the shapes resulting from throwing a handful of soil on a flat surface.

Geomancy, astrological: A system of divination, employing a map containing twelve divisions, in which are placed symbols of geomancy, in conjunction with the ruling planets and signs.

Geoarc: A term applied by some modern astrologers to one of the house divisions of a map erected for a given moment, when considering the effect upon an individual, at a given point on the Earth's periphery, of his motion around the Earth's center—in the Earth's daily rotation. The same subdivision of the same map is called a *heliarc,* when considering effects based on the actual motions in orbit around the Sun, of all the planets—including the Earth. In other words, Geoarc is synonymous with *House,* and Heliarc with *Solar House,* emphasizing the character of the motion to which the subdivisions apply.

Gharb i mutlaq: Arabic for the *absolute void;* in Sufism, the plane of absolute inactual being.

Ghebers: See: *Gabars.*

Ghost: In mediumistic terminology, a deceased person or the image of a deceased person appearing to the living. Identified by occultists with the *astral shell* or *etheric double* (q.v.).

Ghost cult: The practices and ritual observances, associated with the propitiation or avoidance of the ghosts of the dead.

Ghost-seer: A person able to see discarnate spirits. In the folklore of most nations, persons born on certain days or at certain times of the day are credited with this faculty.

Ghostway ceremonials: Magic rites of the Navajo Indians.

Ghoul: A demon which feeds on dead bodies of human beings.

Ginnunga gap: The primeval chaos from which, according to old Norse mythology, all things issued. (The term has been variously translated as *yawning gap, gaping void,* etc.)

Girru: The Babylonian god of fire.

Gligua: Medicine-man or witch-doctor of Chilean Indians.

Glossolalia: The speaking in unknown or non-existent tongues. (See: *Xenoglossis.*)

Glottologue: A medium who speaks in unknown tongues. (See: *Xenoglossis.*)

Gnana, etc. See: *Jnana,* etc.

Gnome: An *elemental* (q.v.) of the element Earth.

Gnosiology: Theory of knowledge in so far as it relates to the origin, nature, limits and validity of knowledge as distinguished from methodology, the study of the basic concepts, postulates and presuppositions of the special sciences.

Gnosis: Greek for *knowledge.* Originally, a generic term for knowledge, in the first and second centuries A.D. it came to mean an esoteric knowledge of higher religious and philosophic truths to be acquired by an elite group of intellectually developed believers. (See: *Gnosticism.*)

Gnosticism: A creed representing a mixture of the doctrines of the Babylonian, Egyptian, Indian and Christian religions, occultism, astrology and magic, as well as parts of the Hebrew Kabalistic teachings. Its origin is still a matter of debate. According to the *Encyclopedia of Religion* by V. Ferm, "Gnosticism is now regarded as pre-Christian Oriental mysticism." All Gnostic sects had their priests who practiced astrology and the magic arts, and it is claimed that the Gnostics continued to celebrate the ancient Greek mysteries, too. The Church regarded the Gnostics as heretics and sorcerers and persecuted them as such.

Goat: The form in which the devil was supposed to preside over the Witches' Sabbath. (See: *Bachelor; Baphomet.*) (For the astrological significance of the word, see *Capricorn.*)

Goblin: A mischievous nature-spirit.

Godhead: In general, the state of being a god, godhood, godness, divinity, deity. More strictly, the essential nature of God, especially the triune God, the One in Three.

Goëtic magic: Black magic, sorcery.

Gog and Magog: In Hebrew occultism, the rebel people who rise up against God and His anointed.

Golden age: In occultism, the *Satya Yuga* (q.v.); an era of purity, simplicity of interests and pursuits and universal happiness.

Golden chain: See: *Hermetic chain.*

Golem: In Jewish mystic lore, an android or homunculus (q.v.) made by the great medieval mystic Rabbi Loew of Prague, who wrote the ineffable name of God on a piece of parchment which he placed in the android's mouth; the magic name gave the Golem life and it was alive until the parchment was removed, when it again became an empty, lifeless hulk.

Gomerah: The medicine-man or shamanistic medium of certain tribes of Australian aborigines.

Good Wisdom, Stage of: See: *Dasa-bhumi.*

Gorgons: In Greek mythology, three hideous sisters, with serpent-entwined hair and glaring eyes that turned to stone anything that met their gaze.

Grail: See: *Holy Grail.*

Grand trine: In astrology, two planets trine (q.v.) to each other, both of which are trined by a third planet.

Graphology: The study of the relations between a person's handwriting and his character.

Greal: In the myths of the early inhabitants of the British Isles, a magic drink, supposed to give inspiration and enlightenment, prepared by the fertility goddess Ceridwen from the juices of six plants.

Great change: Since all occult philosophies believe in survival after the death of the physical body, and hence according to them there is really no death, physical death is usually referred to as the *great change* or the *transition.*

Great Circle of Necessity: The Orphic term for the Wheel of

Life, the alternations of life and death, of imprisonment in a physical body and freedom.

Great Initiate: See: *Elder Brother.*

Great terrestrial crucible: See: *Astral light.*

Great White Brotherhood: In general occult terminology, a synonym for Great White Lodge (q.v.). In the terminology of the Rosicrucians, the Great White Brotherhood is "the school or *Fraternity* of the Great White Lodge and into this invisible Brotherhood of *visible* members every true student of the Path prepares for admission." (Rosicrucian Manual)

Great White Lodge: The Hierarchy of Adepts or Elder Brothers which, according to occultistic teachings, is the true, inner government of the world.

Greater mysteries: The *solar mysteries* (q.v.).

Green Lion, Hunting of the: A medieval alchemical treatise on the search for the Philosopher's Stone (q.v.). The Green Lion is natural, unpurified, undeified Man—green because he is unripe, his occult powers are dormant, but having the strength and fierceness of a lion.

Grhya-sutras: The "House Books" of Hinduism, teaching and expounding the rites for the critical points of life, from birth to death, and the family sacrifices.

Grimoire: A name applied to any book on black magic which pretends to teach the practice of black magic, especially the art of the evocation of evil spirits and making an alliance with them.

Gross body: In occult terminology, the physical body.

Group soul: The philosophical concept, introduced by F. W. H. Myers, of a number of souls bound together by one spirit, acting and reacting upon each other in the ascending scale of psychic evolution.

Group spirit: See: *Group soul.*

Gruagach: A benevolent but mischievous fairy of Scottish folklore.

Guardian angel: Synonym for *guide* (q.v.).

Guide: While this term is frequently used in spiritualism and occultism in general as a synonym for *control* (q.v.), properly used it means a continual, benevolent, protective supermundane influence. (*Control* may be any communicator who happens to make contact with a medium.)

Guiding spirit: Synonym for *guide* (q.v.).

Guna: A Sanskrit term denoting a quality or basic attribute of the Cosmic Substance (*prakriti*). The three *gunas* of *prakriti* are: *sattva, rajas* and *tamas* (q.v.).

Gupta Vidya: Sanskrit for *esoteric knowledge.*

Guru: The Sanskrit term for *spiritual leader* or *teacher.*

Gyromancy: Divination by having a person walk around a chalked circle until he collapses and observing the position of his body relative to the circle.

H

Haborym: In demonography, the demon of fires, a "Duke of the infernal empire."

Hades: In Greek mythology the god of the underworld, the son of Cronos and Rhea and the brother of Zeus; hence the kingdom ruled over by Hades, or the abode of the dead.

Hagith: The Olympian Spirit (q.v.) governing Venus, ruler of 21 Olympian Provinces of the universe; his day is Friday.

Hallucination: A non-veridical or delusive perception of a sense object occurring when no object is in fact present to the organs of sense. (Cf. *negative hallucination.*) In occultistic and esoteric terminology, a state following a relaxation of the nervous system which attracts waves of astral light to the individual who thus may temporarily acquire and use *extrasensory* or *extratemporal perception* (q.v.).

Halomancy: Divination by interpreting the significance of the shapes taken by salt thrown on a flat surface.

Hamadryad: In Greco-Roman mythology, a nature-spirit of the woods, which lives in and dies with a certain tree.

Handatar; handandatar: See: *Para handatar.*

Haoma: In Mazdaism and Parsism, a sacramental drink, prepared by the priests from the juice of the haoma plant with milk and water. It typifies the drink of immortality, yet to come to the faithful.

Harmony of the spheres: See: *Music of the spheres.*

Harpy: In classical mythology, a monstrous, evil, rapacious and vengeful creature with the head and breasts of a woman, the body of a bird and the claws of a lion.

Haruspicy: See: *Aruspicy.*

Harvest festivals: Festival held at harvest time, originating from ancient commemorations of the annual death of grain and vegetation, when the Earth Mother or her child withdraws into the underworld and fertility and growth are suspended on the earth.

Hasid: A Hebrew word (plural: *Hasidim*), meaning *pious,* originally denoting a Jewish mystic and practitioner of esoteric science. The *Hasidim* of the 18th and 19th centuries strove for a spiritual and mystic revival in Judaism.

Hasidism: The philosophic doctrine and movement of the Hasidim.

Hathayoga: Yoga in its aspect of physical health discipline.

Hathor: The cow goddess of ancient Upper Egypt, cow goddess of the sky which gives birth to the sun; the sky conceived as an immense cow with legs planted at the four corners of the earth, and upheld by the other gods.

Hatif: In pre-Islamic Arabic folklore, an invisible nature-spirit who can be heard by men as he gives advice and warnings.

Haunted house, place, etc.: A house, etc., where the same ghostly apparition can be seen, usually at the same hour, every day, or whenever someone enters. One of the principal objects of psychical research.

Haurvatat: In Zoroastrianism, one of the six Amesha Spentas (q.v.), personified representation of "saving health," spirit of the waters.

Heaven-world: The designation used by certain schools of occultism for the *mental plane* of existence.

Heavenly Man: *Adam Kadmon* (q.v.).

Hecate: In ancient Greek mythology, a goddess of magicians and sorcerers, commander of all magic powers of nature.

Hedonism: A term derived from the Greek *hedone* (pleasure), used as a general name for ethical and psychological theories which make pleasure the aim of conduct and behavior.

Heliarc: See: *Geoarc.*

Hepatoscopy: A form of divination, by studying the liver of a sacrificed sheep, practiced among the Babylonians, Etruscans, Hittites, etc., based on the assumption that the seat of life is in the liver, and that the structure of the world and the fortune of the individual may be traced on the liver of the animal.

Heptad: In numerology, the number Seven.

Hera: In Greek mythology, the sister and wife of Zeus, queen of the gods, goddess of marriage.

Hermes: The ancient Greek god of herds, guardian of travellers, messenger of the gods, conductor of the dead to the underworld. The Romans identified him with Mercury. In Egypt, he was identified with Hermanubis, and chiefly with Thoth, the god of learning, and in the Roman imperial period he was worshipped as a revealer of divine wisdom by which men may become a new man, a Son of God.

Hermes Trismegistus: The fabled author of Neo-Platonic, Judaic, Kabalistic, alchemical and astrological works, studied as sacred writings by the Egyptian priests. Identified with the Egyptian god Thoth.

Hermetic: An adjective originally meaning "originated by Hermes Trismegistus or based on his teachings." Now used to mean occult or esoteric in general. (Also: *hermetical.*) Used also as a noun meaning a student or practitioner of alchemy or occultism or esoteric science.

Hermetic chain: In occult teachings, a mystic chain of living entities, starting with the divine beings, and running through the demigods and sages to ordinary human beings, ending in the beings on the lower evolutionary levels.

Hermetist: A follower and propagator of the teachings of Hermes Trismegistus.

Hesperus: The classical name of the planet Venus when appearing after sunset.

Hestia: In Greek mythology, sister of Zeus, virgin goddess of the hearth, both of the home and of the city from which each group of colonists would take sacred fire to its new home.

Heuristic: Serving to find out, helping to show how the qualities and relations of objects are to be sought.

Hexad: In numerology, the number Six.

Hierarchy of Adepts: See: *Great White Lodge.*

Hierophant: Greek for *demonstrator of sacred matters.* The ancient title of higher adepts and teachers of the classical mysteries. Currently used by occultists as a title of initiators into esoteric knowledge.

Higher triad: In occult philosophy, the vital soul, the animal soul and the rationalized soul.

Hinduism: A broad term designating the traditional religious and philosophic systems of India, past and present. (Cf. *Vedic Hinduism; Brahmanic Hinduism.*)

Hippomancy: Divination by observing the gait of horses.

Hiranyagarbha: Sanskrit for *golden germ.* The Cosmic Intelligence or Soul of the Universe. (See: *World Soul.*)

Hobgoblin: A cheerful but very mischievous fairy or nature-spirit who delights in playing pranks on mortal beings.

Hocus-pocus: An expression believed to have magic power. (Probably derived from the Latin *hoc est corpus,* "this is the body," of the Catholic ritual.)

Holy Grail: A vessel of utmost sacredness, the quest for which is the subject of many tales, legends and myths. The Holy Grail and the tales built around it indubitably have a mystic, symbolical significance.

Homunculus: An artificially produced human being. (Plural: *Homunculi.*) The alchemists were reputed to master the art of producing *homunculi.*

Horary astrology: That branch or school of astrology which endeavors to interpret the relationship between cosmic phenomena resulting from the ordered motions of the celestial bodies, and a thought, situation or event. It is considered to be able to deal successfully only with concrete, well-defined queries, and its validity is regarded as subject to question when the particular problem to be analyzed is hazy in the mind of the querent, or ill-defined in its presentation to the astrologer.

Horoscope: As generally employed in astrology, this term refers to the Figure, or Map of the Heavens, for a given date and hour, utilized by astrologers for the judgment of a Nativity and for predictions in Mundane and Horary Astrology; also delineations based thereon. In astrological parlance a Day Horoscope is a horoscope cast for a birth moment in which the Sun was above the horizon, hence in one of the Houses numbered from 7 to 12; a Night Horoscope is one in which the Sun is below the horizon, in a House numbered between 1 and 6.

Horse-whispering: A magical art of taming wild horses by whispering certain secret magical formulas into their ears.

Horus: A sun and war god of ancient Egypt, son of Osiris and Isis.

Hotar: Sanskrit for *caller*. Priest-magicians who invoke the gods by reciting ritual formulas and improvised chants.

Houris: The maidens who cater to the faithful in the Islamic Paradise.

House: An astrological Figure is divided into 12 arcs, equal either in terms of space or time. If in terms of space the arcs are of 30° each, one twelfth of the circle of 360°. If the subdivision begins at a given moment, and each division represents the celestial arc that passes over the horizon in 2 hours—one twelfth of the time required for one complete rotation—the divisions are known as Houses. (If the arcs begin at 0° Aries they are known as the Signs of the Zodiac, from Aries to Pisces, and represent subdivisions of the orbit of the Earth round the Sun. As such they are *Signs*, not Houses.)

House Books: See: *Grhya-sutras.*

Hsiao: In Chinese philosophy, filial piety; love of parents; serving and supporting one's parents in the best way. It is "the standard of Heaven, the principle of Earth, and the basis for the conduct of Man," "the basis of morality and the root of culture."

Hsin chai: Chinese for *fasting of the mind*. A state of pure experience in which one has no intellectual knowledge, in which there is immediate presentation; the attainment of the mystical state of unity. (Chuang Tzu, between 399 and 295 B.C.)

Hsing: In Chinese philosophy, the nature of man and things, especially human nature, understood as "what is inborn," or "what is created." It is what is imparted by Heaven, whereas what is received by man and things is fate (*ming*). The original state of the nature is tranquil. In its aroused state, when it comes into contact with the external world, it becomes feelings (*ch'ing*).

Hsuan chiao: Chinese for *the Doctrine of Mystery*, another name for the Taoist religion.

Hsu wu: A Chinese term for emptiness and non-existence referring to Tao which is so full and real that it appears to be empty and non-existent. "It is in the empty and the non-existent where Tao is found."

Huaca: An oracle of the Peruvian Indians.

Human sacrifice: The ceremonial killing of a human being as an offering to a god or for other mystical or magical purposes.

Human signs: The designation applied by astrologers to the signs Gemini, Virgo, Aquarius, and to the first half of Sagittarius.

Hun: The Chinese term for the active, positive or heavenly part of the soul, as contrasted with the passive, negative or earthly part of the soul, which is called *p'o*.

Hun mang: The Taoist conception of the Golden Age, in which there was in the beginning, in the time of the primeval chaos, a state of absolute harmony between man and his surroundings, a life as effortless and spontaneous as the passage of the seasons, the two cosmic principles of *yin* and *yang* worked together instead of in opposition.

Huntin: An African tree spirit.

Hurtful signs: In astrology, the signs Aries, Taurus, Cancer, Scorpio, and Capricorn.

Huitzlipochtli: The Aztec god of war, ruler of the Eastern Paradise to which slain warriors were taken.

Huwasi: The Hittite name of upright stones representing gods or consecrated to gods.

Hydromancy: Divination by water.

Hyle: The first primordial substance, out of which the material universe was formed.

Hyleg: In astrology, a designation applied to a planet so located as to have influence upon the longevity of the native. It is one of the most complex and controversial subjects in the field of astrology, but now has fallen more or less in disfavor. The strongest planet that occupied one of the Aphetic places became Hyleg, and was deemed to be the Apheta, the *giver of life*. When it had progressed to an aspect to the place of the Anareta, the taker-away of life, the native was presumed to have run his span and death ensued.

Hylomorphism: A theory that all physical things are constituted of two internal principles: the one of which remains the same throughout all change and is the passive basis of continuity and identity in the physical world, called *prime matter;* the other of which is displaced, or removed from actuation of its matter, in every substantial change, called *substantial form.*

Hylosystemism: A cosmological theory developed by Mitterer principally, which explains the constitution of the natural inorganic body as an atomary energy system.

Hylozoism: The philosophical doctrine that life is a property of matter, that matter and life are inseparable, that life is derived from matter, or that matter has spiritual properties. The conception of nature as alive, or in the words of Thales, that "all things are full of gods."

Hyperborean: The second *root race* (q.v.) in esoteric philosophy.

Hypnotism: "A peculiar state of consciousness, artificially induced, which liberates subconscious powers in the subject, puts him *en rapport* with the hypnotizer, makes him accept and meticulously execute any of his [the hypnotizer's] suggestions, whether hypnotic or post-hypnotic, which do not conflict with deeper instincts of self-preservation and morality, and produces strange psychological effects as anaesthesia and the remarkable control over organic processes of the body. In hypnotic sleep the waking stimuli are strongly resisted, the sleeper hears and answers." (N. Fodor.) Occultists and believers in mysticism consider hypnotism a form of *black magic* (q.v.) unless it is used for expressly beneficial ends.

Hypogeon: (Greek for *under the Earth.*) An all-embracing astrological term generalizing the lower heaven: including the Nadir, the *Imum Cœli,* and the Fourth House.

I

I: In Chinese philosophical terminology: (1) The One, which is engendered by Tao and which in turn engenders the Two (*yin* and *yang*). (Lao Tzu.) (2) Unity of mind, "not allowing one impression to harm another." (3) The number for Heaven, as two is the number for Earth. (4) Righteousness, justice; one of the four Confucian Fundamentals of the Moral Life (*ssu tuan*) and the Five Constant Virtues (*wu ch'ang*). It is the virtue "by which things are made proper," "by which the world is regulated."

I Ching: The Book of Changes (q.v.).

I Yuan: In Chinese philosophy, the One-Prime which is the supreme beginning. It is One and is identical with the Origin. "The Prime is the root of the myriad things, in which there is also the origin of Man." (Tung Chung-shu, 177-104 B.C.)

Iblis: The Moslem equivalent of Satan; the prince of fallen angels who was turned into a devil.

Ichthyomancy: Divination by examining the entrails of fishes.

Ideoplasm: *Ectoplasm* (q.v.) molded into the likeness of a self.

Idol: An image or representation of a supernatural being, in which the latter is believed to have his seat or abode, and before which sacrifices and other acts and rituals of worship are performed.

Idolatry: The worship of a physical object as a god.

Ifrit: A viciously malignant spirit, of hideous appearance, in Arabic folklore.

Igigi: A Babylonian term for the gods or spirits of heaven in general, or specifically, for the gods or spirits embodied in those stars which were above the horizon at any one time.

Ignis fatuus: The luminous appearance frequently observed in marshy places, swamps, cemeteries, etc., explained by spiritualists to be apparitions of spirits of the dead, and by adherents to materialistic science as gaseous emanations.

IHVH: See: *Tetragrammaton.*

Illuminati: The plural of the Latin *illuminatus*, meaning *enlightened one.* While the term is generally used in occultism to designate all those who have "seen the higher light," it has been used in history as a specific designation of various sects and societies, especially the Rosicrucians and the Martinists of the 18th century. A sect under this name was founded by Adam Weishaupt in Germany in 1776.

Illumination, Stage of: See: *Dasa-bhumi.*

Illuminatus: Latin for *enlightened* (plural: *Illuminati*—q.v.). In esoteric terminology, an adept or initiate.

Illusion: An illusion of sense is an erroneous perception arising from a misinterpretation of data of sense because they are produced under unusual conditions of perception, physical, physiological or psychological. Illusion contrasts with hallucination in which the sensuous ingredients are totally absent. In occult terminology, *illusion* is a synonym for *maya* (q.v.), and thus applicable to everything finite.

Image: In Rosicrucian parlance, *to image* means to recollect or to produce mental images. (Not synonymous with *to imagine!*)

Imageless thought: Conceptual meanings not embodied in sensuous imagery.

Imagery: Mental images or sounds heard "within the mind."

Imaging: The Rosicrucian term for the recollection or "reproduction" of mental images. (The verb is *to image.*) Not synonymous with *imagining.*

Imaguncula: An image made of clay, wax, wood, etc., used by practitioners of black magic, witchcraft and sorcery. (Plural: *Imagunculae.*)

Imhetep: An ancient Egyptian god, frequently invoked by magicians to aid in exorcisms.

Imitative magic: Magic based on the belief that things which resemble each other can exert an influence over each other—for instance, that a person can be injured by damaging an effigy made to resemble him.

Immanence: Latin for *in-dwelling*. In general philosophical terminology, this term refers to an activity producing its effects from within, or to an entity whose being within something else contributes to the existence of the latter. In theology, the term refers to the complete or partial identification of the Deity with the world. (The belief in the absolute immanence of God in the universe is equivalent to pantheism.) Mysticism in its broadest sense posits the mutual immanence of the human and the divine.

Immediacy of knowledge: Knowledge gained without mediation, as self-evident or without interpretation and inference.

Immortality: The imperishability of individual existence; survival or reincarnation after the death of the body.

Immovability, Stage of: See: *Dasa-bhumi.*

Immutability: Changelessness, or the state or quality of not being susceptible to any alteration.

Imp: A dwarfish demon. The emissaries of Satan, aiding sorcerers and witches, are usually referred to as *Satanic imps* and are believed to be able to assume any form at will.

Impeded: A synonym for *impedited* (q.v.).

Impedited: An astrological term, applied to a luminary or planet when badly aspected, especially by the malefics. Also said of the Moon when passing to a conjunction, square or opposition to the Sun, Mars, or Saturn. (The Moon when impedited by the Sun at birth was believed by the ancients to produce a blemish in or near the eye.)

Impersonation: Imitation of a deceased person by a medium, by assuming his physical characteristics, voice and mannerisms.

Imum Cœli: In astrological terminology, the lowest heaven, the North Angle or cusp of the Fourth House.

Inari: Deities of food and fertility in Shintoism.

Incantation: Any phrase or formula spoken, sung or chanted as a part of a ritual of magic.

Incarnate: Living in a physical body.

Incarnation: Life in a physical body; the assumption of a physical body.

Inclination: Astrologically, the motion of a body toward a position in the horoscope other than the one it held at birth.

Inconjunct: Astrologers call a planet inconjunct when it forms no aspect and is not in parallel of declination or mutual disposition to another planet.

Incubus: A term generally applied to designate a demon, astral form of a dead person or of a sorcerer, which has sexual intercourse with mortal women.

Indeterminism: The theory that volitional decisions are in certain cases independent of antecedent physiological and psychological causation.

Individuality: In esoteric philosophy, the divine, impersonal and immortal higher Ego of man.

Indra: The Vedic god of war, storm and fertility, god of the atmosphere and sky, reigning over the deities of the intermediate region or atmosphere.

Indriya: One of five or more sensory functions or "senses," conceived generally in Indian philosophy kinetically as powers subservient to *manas* (q.v.). A common division is into the quintads of *karmendriyas* (q.v.) and *jnanendriyas* (q.v.).

Ineffable Name: In mysticism and occultism, the true name of God which must not be pronounced.

Inescation: The occult medical practice aimed at ridding a human being of an illness by transferring it onto an animal.

Inferior planets: In astrology, the minor planets, those whose orbits are within that of the Earth; viz., Mercury and Venus.

Inferior world: In Kabalistic and occult terminology, the world of matter.

Infernal empire: The term generally used in demonography for the organization of the demons under the rule of Beelzebub, in whose *infernal court* various demons hold ranks of princes, knights, etc.

Infinite: Completely free of limitations, in all respects.

Infinity: An endless extent of space, time, or any series. Is usually conceived negatively, as having no termination; may be conceived positively, in respect to reality as actually extending without end.

Influence: In mediumistic terminology, this term is used as a synonym for "spirit" (in the mediumistic sense of the word).

Information: In scholastic terminology, the function of form when it perfects the matter united to it so as to constitute a specific body. (Cf. *materialization*.)

Infortunes: The term applied by astrologers to the planets Mars and Saturn.

Initiate: One admitted to knowledge of occult mysteries and secrets; one who has acquired occult powers by systematically developing his superphysical capacities.

Initiation: Admission to one of the formal degrees or classifications in an esoteric or occult discipline.

Inner Light: In the terminology of the Society of Friends (Quakers), the capacity inherent in all men to listen to God speaking to the listening soul, to make satisfying spiritual contact with God, and to understand and share spiritual experience.

Inner man: In occult terminology, the immortal essence or higher ego of man.

Inspiration: A state of psychic receptivity to creative spiritual influence.

Integration: The act of making a whole out of parts. In psychology, the combination of psycho-physical elements into a complex unified organization.

Intellect: The cognitive faculty of the mind as it operates at higher abstract and conceptual levels.

Intelligence: The capacity of the mind to meet effectively—through the employment of memory, imagination and conceptual thinking—the practical and theoretical problems with which it is confronted. Intelligence is more inclusive than intellect which is primarily conceptual.

Internal alchemy: The deification of man's spirit.

Internal sense: The mind's ability to scrutinize reflectively its own inner operations.

Interrogation: In occult terminology, the act or practice of consulting an astrologer medium, oracle, etc.

Intichiuma: A rite of natives of central Australia, consisting of ceremonies designed to assure the annual supply of food and drink, including rain-making ceremonies.

Introspection: The observation of the presentations and processes of one's own consciousness.

Insufflation: A practice of occult medicine, consisting in breathing for a certain time upon a person or animal.

Intuition: The faculty or ability to be aware of facts, knowledge of which would or could not be conveyed by normal reasoning processes. The direct and immediate apprehension by a knowing subject of itself, of its conscious states, of other minds, of an external world, of universals, of values or of rational truths.

Invisible fellowship: "The interconnections established among men through common motives and ultimate goals as in contrast with their ties through the structures of a surface society; the subjective side of occult functioning; shared immortality." (Marc Edmund Jones.) See: *Great White Brotherhood.*

Invocation: In the terminology of magic, the act or the formula of calling for the presence of a superhuman entity.

Involution: In occult philosophy, a stage or process which precedes evolution and can be regarded as a process inverse to evolution and as manifesting itself in the *descending arc* (q.v.). "The anterior rolling or coiling which, upon reversal, becomes evolution." (Marc Edmund Jones.) G. A. Gaskell calls it "the descent of Spirit into matter."

Iron Age: The *Kali Yuga* (q.v.).

Irroration: In occult medicine, the practice of watering a plant with the discharge of a sick person, to rid the patient of the disease by transferring it to the plant.

Ishtar: The Babylonian goddess of fertility.

Ishwara: Sanskrit for *independent being*. The personalized God, first stage in the manifestation of Brahman. Ishwara manifests himself in three aspects: *Brahma*, the Creator, *Vishnu*, the Preserver, and *Shiva*, the Destroyer.

Isis: Wife of Osiris, greatest of all goddesses of ancient Egypt, "the Great Enchantress, the Mistress of Magic, the Speaker of Spells."

Isis-Osiris mysteries: Egyptian mysteries (q.v.) which were practiced widely around the Mediterranean, commemorating the death and resurrection of Osiris.

Iswara: See: *Ishwara.*

J

Jadi-jadian: The were-tiger of Malay folklore, a counterpart of the werewolf of European races.

Jaggannath: Sanskrit for *lord of the world*. A variant name of Vishnu, the Preserver, under which he is worshipped in Puri. The most notable feature of his worship is the "car festival," in which a great car bearing a huge image of Jaggannath is hauled by thousands of worshippers from his temple to the Garden House, some four miles away. In former days, many worshipers would hurl themselves under the huge wheels, to be crushed to death. (Also called *Juggernaut*.)

Jagrat: In Hindu metaphysical and occult philosophy, the lowest quality of consciousness, that of waking activity in which man is passively subject to the impositions of a world of artificial and deceptive images.

Jaina cross: The *swastika* (q.v.).

Jainism: An Indian religion claiming great antiquity, the last of the great teachers (*tirthankara*) being Mahavira (6th century B.C.), embracing many philosophical elements of a pluralistic type of realism. It rejects Vedic (q.v.) authority and an absolute being, gods as well as men partaking of mortality, and holds the mythologically conceived world to be eternal and subject only to the fixed sequence of six ages, good and bad, but not periodic creation and destruction. There is an infinitude of indestructible individual souls or spiritual entities, each possessing by nature many properties inclusive of omniscience, unlimited energy and bliss which come to the fore upon attaining full independence. The nonspiritual substances are space and time, rest and motion, and matter composed of atoms and capable of being apprehended by the senses and combining to form the world of infinite variety. Matter also penetrates spiritual substances like a physician's pill, changing to *karma* and producing physical attachments.

Janus: The Roman god of the doorway; two-faced, he became the god of the beginnings.

Japa: Sanskrit for *invocation*.

Jehovah: (From the Hebrew *Yahveh*, of doubtful origin and meaning.) Personal name of God or the supreme being in Hebrew theological and philosophical writings, common only since the 14th century; the national god of Israel since Mosaic times. Neither name was originally pronounced as written on account of its holiness, but was replaced by *Elohim* and *Adonai*.

Jemalang: The earth-spirit of the Malays.

Jen: In Chinese: (1) Man, (2) manhood, (3) moral character, (4) love, kindness, charity, compassion, benevolence.

Jerusalem of above: In Jewish mysticism, the heavenly counterpart of the city of Jerusalem on Earth.

Jetzirah: See: *Yetzirah*.

JHVH: See: *Tetragrammaton*.

Jihad: A religious war of Moslems against unbelievers; also a war or crusade for or against some doctrine or principle. (The Admadiya sect of Islam interprets *jihad* as a striving after righteousness.)

Jinn; jinnee: In Arab occultistic terminology, one of a race of beings created out of fire, which inhabited the Earth before the advent of man. They can become visible or invisible at will, have many other superhuman and magic powers. Some *jinns* are good and friendly to humans, others are malignant.

Jiva: A Sanskrit term for the principle of life, the individual soul as distinguished from the Universal Soul (*purusha*).

Jivakosa: In Hindu mysticism, a case or sheath which envelops the personal soul.

Jivanmukta: A Sanskrit term, denoting one who has attained salvation while in this present life: all but a remainder of *prarabdha karma* has been neutralized and no new *karma* is accumulated in virtue of the person's having gained insight, *jnana* (q.v.).

Jnana: Sanskrit for *knowledge* or *spiritual enlightenment*.

Jnana-marga: Sanskrit for *path of knowledge*. The approach to spiritual perfection through spiritual knowledge and understanding.

Jnanendriya: A Sanskrit term for one of the five *indriyas* (q.v.) of knowledge, the cognitive senses or powers of hearing, seeing, feeling, smelling, and tasting.

Jnani: Sanskrit for *savant*—said of a man who has acquired full spiritual enlightenment.

Jötunn: In Norse-Icelandic mythology, a giant or earth monster.

Jötunheim: The home of the Jötunns (q.v.) in Norse-Icelandic mythology.

Jou: Chinese for *weakness;* the principle of weakness, opposite of the principle of strength; the outstanding characteristic of the Earthly Principle (*k'un*) and corresponding to the passive cosmic principle (*yin*).

Jove: One of the names under which the Roman god Jupiter was worshipped.

Joy, Stage of: See: *Dasa-bhumi*.

Joy: A term employed by some of the older astrologers to indicate an affinity between certain planets and certain Signs.

Ju Chia: Chinese for *School of the Learned*. The Confucian School, which "delighted in the study of the six Classics and paid attention to matters concerning benevolence and righteousness."

Ju Chiao: Chinese for *Teaching of the Learned*. The teachings of the Confucian school, based on the Confucian classics with the chief emphasis on ethics and polity. Since the establishment of Confucianism as the state cult in the second century A.D., the term has also been used to designate the traditional system of worship of Shang Ti, ancestors, etc., which the Confucians followed.

Ju ju: African native witchcraft.

Judicial Astrology: A term synonymous with *Mundane Astrology* (q.v.).

Juggernaut: See: *Jaggannath*.

Juno: In Roman mythology, wife of Jupiter, queen of the gods, mistress of heaven and earth, patroness of marriage and female virtue.

Jupiter: Chief deity, lord of heaven and earth, king of the gods of the Romans. Identified with Zeus of the Greeks.

Jupiter-Ammon: The Roman god Jupiter identified with the Egyptian deity Amon; his statue was said to give spoken oracles.

Jurupari: An evil deity worshipped by the Uapé Indians of Brazil.

K

Ka: The ancient Egyptian term for the *astral body* (q.v.), conceived of as the guardian and companion of the soul both in the physical body and in the after-life.

Kabalah: The esoteric mystic lore of Judaism, based on an occult interpretation of the Bible and handed down as a secret doctrine to the initiated. It is an essential element in most schools of occultism.

Kabbala; Kabbalah: See: *Kabalah.*

Kabeiri: See: *Cabiri.*

Kagyud: A semi-reformed sect of Lamaism (Tibetan Buddhism); called the White Sect.

Kaid-mords: The first man according to Persian mystics.

Kalevala: The Finnish epic of creation.

Kali: Hindu goddess of time, wife of Shakti or Shiva, said to be the Mother, creator of all things. The personification of cosmic force.

Kali yuga: The dark age of Hindu mythology, last *yuga* of the current *manvantara* (q.v.); it began at midnight between the 17th and 18th of February 3102 B.C.; it is a fourth less righteous and briefer than the preceding, enduring 432,000 years (one-tenth of the entire *manvantara*); it is characterized by strife, discord, quarreling, and contention; at the end of this age the world is to be destroyed.

Kalpa: A day and a night of Brahma, consisting of 4,320,000,000 of our years.

Kama Rupa: A Sanskrit term used in metaphysics and esoteric philosophy to designate a subjective, astral form which lives on after the death of the physical body; an *eidolon*. The Kama Rupa is believed to fade away and disintegrate gradually, although necromantic practices and ardent wishes of surviving kin may draw it back into the terrestrial sphere and extend its existence, causing it to become a vampire which feeds on the life force of those who called it back.

Kama-loka: The Sanskrit name of the semi-material plane which is the dwelling place of the *Kama Rupa* (q.v.).

Kami: A Japanese word translated as *deity, god, goddess,* etc. The original significance of *kami* is *occult power,* more or less like the meaning of *mana* (q.v.).

Kaph: In Arabic myths, encountered also among most Moslem peoples of the East, the great circular mountain which completely surrounds the Earth and is the dwelling place of nature-spirits.

Karma: Sanskrit for *action* or *deed.* In Hinduism and occult philosophy, the dynamic manifestation of mental and physical energy in deeds, speech or thought which inevitably produces a good, evil or indifferent effect, according as the action is good, evil or indifferent, and the effect itself becomes the cause of further effects. Thus *karma* is the law of physical causation or cause and effect, the unmitigated law of retribution, working with equal precision in good and evil thoughts and deeds, thus determining the nature and circumstances of man's future incarnation. Thus *karma* is (1) action-energy, past or present, latent or manifest, actual or potential; (2) a self-operating law of cause and effect and retribution; (3) the entity of the individual or of the universe carried along in the series of the Wheel of Life (*samsara*).

Karma-marga: Sanskrit for *path of action.* The term applied in Hindu philosophy to the approach to God and spiritual perfection through selfless and harmonious actions (cf. *Karma; karma yoga*).

Karma yoga: The quest of the mystic union with the Divine Spirit through the *karma-marga,* consecrated action; complete control of one's personality is sought, in order to subdue its self-conscious, self-centered desires, so as to make one's actions cosmocentric, in complete harmony with the purposes of the universal One.

Karmendriya: In Hinduism and occult philosophy, one of the five *indriyas* (q.v.) or powers of action, reactive or muscular senses, corresponding to the physiological capacities of expression or speech, seizing or handling, locomotion, excretion, and sexual activity.

Karmic: Relating to or having the characteristics of the effects of Karma (q.v.).

Katcinas: Supernatural beings in the cosmology of the Hopi Indians.

Kavod: A Hebrew Kabalistic term for *Divine Glory*.

Kavvanah: A Hebrew mystical term, meaning *intention* or *devotion*. (Plural: *Kavvanoth*.) "The intention directed towards God while performing a (religious) deed. In the Kabbalah, *kavvanoth* denote the permutations of the divine name that aim at overcoming the separation of forces in the Upper World." (M. Buber.) The word means also a devoted prayer delivered with great concentration.

Kelpie: A mischievous water spirit. Kelpies are believed in Scotland to haunt rivers, waterfalls, etc.

Kevala: Sanskrit for *alone*. A predicate or synonym of the Absolute in its unitary, free, autonomous, all-inclusive and universal aspect. The condition or state of being absolute and independent is *kevalatva;* one who meditates or has attained personal experience of it, is a *kevalin.*

Key of Solomon the King: A treatise on magic, dating probably from the 14th or 15th century, although it pretends to have been written by King Solomon. (Cf. *Lemegeton.*)

Keys of the tarot: The twenty-two *major arcana* of the *tarot* deck (q.v.).

Khaibit: In Egyptian occultism, the third member of the higher triad: *Ka*, the astral body, *Ba*, the soul, and *Khaibit*, the *shadow*.

Kherbet: Magician-priest of ancient Egypt.

Kingu: Babylonian god of the powers of darkness and black magic.

Kishuph: In Hebrew Kabalistic terminology, magic and its effects.

Kismet: Arabic for *fate;* a word frequently used by Moslems, to express their belief in a fate that rules the affairs of men and preordains and makes inevitable man's fortunes and deeds, with their future consequences.

Kiva: A subterranean or semi-subterranean ceremonial chamber in Pueblo Indian villages, used mainly and especially for religious rites of mystic significance.

Klippoth: The "world of shells" of Kabalistic cosmogony, formed from the emanations of the Yetzirah (q.v.).

Kneph: The ram-headed god, creator of the universe in Egyptian mythology.

Knife-edge present: That part of time called *present*, conceived as having no duration.

Knights Templar: See: *Templars*.

K'o chi: A Chinese term which may be translated as conquering, controlling oneself or self-cultivation, Chinese scholars being divided in interpretation. By the first interpretation it means "restoring the moral order" and being a true man *(jen)*, avoiding, in particular, partiality and selfish desires. By the second interpretation it means self-realization.

Kobold: A mischievous nature spirit, living in caves and subterranean places.

Koji-ki: The oldest extant Japanese historical document, compiled in 712 A.D. It begins with the myth of Creation and ends with 628 A.D.

Kosa: Sanskrit for *sheath*. One of the envelopes of the soul or self concealing its real nature, which is pure consciousness. The Vedanta knows three: the *anandamaya, vijnanamaya,* and *annamaya kosas,* i.e., the sheaths of pleasure, intellect, and food, composing respectively the *karana, suksma,* and *sthula sharira,* meaning the causal, subtle, and gross frame or body.

Krishna: The eighth Avatar (reincarnation of Vishnu) of Hindu mythology and occultism, whose teachings are recorded in the Bhagavad Gita.

Krita yuga: A synonym for *satya yuga* (q.v.).

Kru: A shaman of Cambodia (Indo-China).

Kshathra: One of the six Amesha Spentas (q.v.) of Zoroastrianism, personified representation of rulership, spirit of metals.

Kuai: The Chinese name for spirits of non-human beings and inanimate objects.

Kuei: Chinese for *spirit of human being*, used especially in the meaning "ancestor."

Kurumba: The shamanistic medicine-man of certain primitive tribes of Southern India.

L

Lakshmi: The Hindu goddess of fortune and beauty, wife of Vishnu.

Lama: A Tibetan priest or monk and student and practitioner of esoteric science and occult arts.

Lamaism: A popular term for Tibetan esoteric Buddhism, not used by the Buddhists themselves. It designates the religious beliefs and institutions of Tibet, derived from Mahayana Buddhism (q.v.) which was first introduced in the seventh century by the chieftain Sron-tsan-gampo, superimposed on the native Shamaistic Bon religion, resuscitated and mixed with Tantric (q.v.) elements by the mythic Hindu Padmasambhava, and reformed by the Bengalese Atisa in the 11th and Tsong-kha-pa at the turn of the 14th century. The strong admixture of elements of the exorcismal, highly magically charged and priest-ridden original Bon, has given Buddhism a turn away from its philosophic orientation and produced in Lamaism a form that places great emphasis on *mantras* (q.v.)—the most famous one being *om mani padme hum* —elaborate ritual, and the worship of subsidiary tutelary deities, high dignitaries, and living incarnations of the Buddha. This worship is institutionalized, incorporating a belief in the double incarnation of the Bodhisattva (q.v.) in the Dalai-Lama who resides with political powers at the capital Lhasa, and the more spiritual head Tashi-Lama who rules at Tashi-lhum-po.

Lamia: A demon, believed to assume the form of a beautiful woman and devour children or suck their blood. (Plural: *lamiae* or *lamias*.)

Lampadomancy: Divination using the flame of a lamp as source of omens.

Lapis exilis: The magical stone which enables the phoenix to regain its youth. Some authors hold the view that *lapis exilis* was a synonym for the Holy Grail (q.v.).

Lapis philosophorum: Latin for Philosopher's Stone (q.v.).

Lares: Spirits of the fields in Roman mythology. Usually associated and invoked with the *Lares*, the household spirits.

Larva: In occultism, a visible manifestation of the *astral shell* or *etheric double* (q.v.).

Law of Retribution: Karma (q.v.), the Law of Ethical Causation.

Laya-center: "The mystical *point* where a thing disappears from one plane and passes onwards to reappear on another plane. . . . the point where substance rebecomes homogeneous. Any laya-center, therefore, of necessity exists in and on the critical line or stage dividing one plane from another." (G. de Purucker, *Occult Glossary*, Theosophical University Press, 1953.)

Laya yoga: That school of Yoga which seeks union with the Divine Spirit through his operations on the etheric plane, by becoming conscious of the Divine presence in the operations tending to keep our being in manifestation. Certain incantations are supposed to operate through their capacity to create centers of harmony on the etheric plane and to induce a corresponding harmony in the successively more spiritual centers of the four internal mental organs (*antahkarana*).

Laying on of hands: A method used by a qualified person to transmit powers or authority to another.

Lecanomancy: Divination by throwing an object in a basin full of water and interpreting the image of that object in the water or the sound of its fall.

Leffas: In occult terminology, the astral bodies (q.v.) of plants.

Left: In the terminology of occultism, the use of occult powers for evil or improper purposes; black magic. (Cf. *brother of the left-hand path*.)

Legate: In occult terminology, the designation of one formally initiated into the *invisible fellowship* (q.v.).

Legend: Traditions of slow growth, embodying popular feeling and consisting of mixtures of fact and fancy which are presented as historical.

Legomena: Esoteric knowledge taught by spoken word. (The term originates from the Eleusinian mysteries.)

Leippya: In Burmese occult lore, the invisible butterfly, in the shape of which the soul of the dead hovers in the vicinity of the body.

Lemegeton: A textbook of ceremonial magic, conjuration, etc. (Frequently referred to also as the *Lesser Key of Solomon.*) It probably was compiled in the 17th century A.D.

Lemures: In occultism, elementals (q.v.) of the air, or elementaries (q.v.) of the deceased. "Rapping and table-tilting spirits," producing physical manifestations.

Lemuria: The "lost continent" of the third *root race* (q.v.) according to esoteric philosophy; also known as *Mu.*

Lemurian: The third *root race* (q.v.) in esoteric philosophy.

Leo (The Lion): The fifth sign of the zodiac. Its symbol (♌) is possibly an emblem representing the phallus, as used in ancient Dionysian mysteries. It is also an emblem of the Sun's fire, heat or creative energy. The Sun is in Leo annually from July 23 to August 22. Astrologically it is the second thirty-degree arc after the Summer Solstice, marked by the Sun's passing of the Tropic of Cancer and occupying a position along the Ecliptic from 120° to 150°. It is the "fixed" quality of the element Fire, conferring an internal will motivated by an impulse of the heart. It is positive, hot, dry, choleric, eastern, diurnal, commanding, brutish, sterile, broken, changeable, fortunate, strong, hoarse, bitter, and violent. Ruler: Sun. Detriment: Saturn. Fall: Mercury. Leo exemplifies the principle of cosmic splendor.

Leprechaun: Nature-spirits of Irish occult lore.

Lesser Key of Solomon: See: *Lemegeton.*

Lesser mysteries: That part of the ancient *mysteries* (q.v.). consisting mainly of rites and ceremonies.

Level: A grade or type of existence or being which entails a special type of relatedness or of organization, with distinctive laws. The term has been used primarily in connection with theories of emergent evolution where certain so-called higher levels, e.g. life, or mind, are supposed to have emerged from the lower levels, e.g. matter, and are considered to exhibit features of novelty not predictable from the lower levels.

Levitation: The raising of the human body or other physical object into the air, without any visible means to produce or maintain this effect, and contrary to the laws of gravitation.

Libra (The Balances, or Scales): The seventh sign of the zodiac. Its symbol (♎), representing the balancing scales, is emblematic of equilibrium and justice. The Sun is in Libra annually from September 23 to October 23. Astrologically it is the first thirty-degree arc following the passing of the Sun over the Fall Equinoctial point, occupying a position along the Ecliptic from 180° to 210°. It is the "leading" quality of the element Air: positive, hot, moist, sweet, obeying: also restless, judicial. Ruler: Venus. Exaltation: Saturn. Detriment: Mars. Fall: Sun. Symbolic interpretation: The setting Sun; the central part of a balance, signifying equilibrium and justice.

Life stream: In occult terminology, the entirety of humanity, including both those now living in physical bodies and those discarnate.

Light of grace: Cf. *Lumen naturae.*

Light of nature: See: *Lumen naturae.*

Lights: A term frequently applied in astrology to the Luminaries (the Sun and Moon as distinguished from the planets).

Lilith: In Jewish mysticism, a female demon who seduces mortal men. (Cf. *succubus.*) Specifically, the first wife of Adam before the creation of Eve.

Ling chos: Tibetan legends and tales of gods, demons and giants; parts of an ancient pre-Buddhist religion, carried on in the folklore of the peoples of Tibet.

Linga; lingam: The phallic symbol under which Shiva is almost universally worshipped in India. It represents fertility and regenerative power.

Lingasharira: Sanskrit name of the *etheric double* (q.v.).

Lion: See: *Leo.*

Lithomancy: Divination by observing precious stones.

Localization, cerebral: The supposed correlation of mental processes, sensory and motor, with definite areas of the brain. The theory of definite and exact brain localization has been largely disproven by recent physiological investigations.

Logos: A Greek term for the manifested effect of a hidden cause. In the mystic sense in general, the cosmic law and order. In theosophical terminology, the manifested Deity, "whose speech is thought."

Loki: A Norse god of varying character, cunning, skillful, artistic, but treacherous; able to assume human form.

Lord: A term often used in astrology synonymously with Ruler. A more precise terminology would be to refer to the *Ruler* of a *Sign* and the *Lord* of a *House.*

Lord of Civilization, The: In occult literature, the *Mahachohan* (q.v.).

Loup-garou: French for *werewolf* (q.v.).

Lotus sutra: The most popular Buddhist scriptures in the Orient, which teaches salvation for all creatures and propounds the principle that "One is All and All is One."

Lower quaternary: In occult terminology, the physical body, the etheric double, the astral body, and the mental body (q.v.).

Lower spirits: The elementals (q.v.).

Lucidity: A collective term for clairvoyance, clairaudience, premonitions, etc.; in general, the faculty which permits one to obtain supernormal knowledge.

Lucifer: In medieval occultism, the name of the devil conceived of as a fallen angel. In classical astronomy and astrology, the name of the planet Venus when appearing in the morning before the sun.

Lucifuge Rofocale: In demonography, the "Prime Minister of the infernal empire."

Lumen naturae; lumen naturale: Latin for *light of nature* or *natural light*, equivalent to *luman naturalis rationis*, in medieval philosophy and theology denoted the ordinary cognitive powers of human reason unaided by the supernatural light of grace, *lumen gratiae*, or divine revelation, *lumen fidei.*

Luminary: In astrological terminology, the Sun or the Moon as distinguished from the planets. (It is an ancient classification hardly in keeping with the fact that the Sun is a direct source of energy, and the light from the Moon, like that from the planets, is reflected from the Sun.)

Luminous arc: See: *ascending arc.*

Luminous body: The Pythagorean term for the *astral body* (q.v.).

Lunar mysteries: The *lesser mysteries* (q.v.).

Lunar pitris: In occultism, the progenitors of human personalities. (See: *pitris.*)

Lunation: As usually employed, a term approximately synonymous with *new moon;* specifically, the precise moment of the moon's conjunction with sun; a syzygy.

Lycanthrophy: The belief that certain human beings, under certain conditions, can change into animals. (See: *Werewolf.*)

Lynx: The living winged globe of Chaldean magic tradition, symbolizing the universal spirit.

M

Maat: The ancient Egyptian goddess of justice. According to Egyptian mythology, the hearts of the deceased were weighed in a balance against an ostrich feather, the symbol of Maat.

Macrocosm: The universe as contrasted with some small part of it which epitomizes it in some respect under consideration or exhibits an analogous structure; in occult philosophy, the Universe or Cosmos, as against Man.

Maggid: Hebrew for *preacher*. (Plural: *Maggidim.*) "The Maggidim were partly itinerant preachers, partly regularly appointed community preachers; some of the latter at times served as wandering preachers. The term also refers to a spirit that appears to the select and reveals to them secrets of the teachings and the future." (M. Buber.)

Magi: The "Wise Ones," philosophers, astrologers and priests of ancient Persia, expounders of Zoroastrian wisdom. Their name is the root of the words *magic, magician,* etc.

Magic: Short for *magic art:* the mastery of occult forces and their use in order to produce visible effects. *White magic* is the use of magic powers for beneficent purposes; *black magic* is the use of supernormal powers in nefarious practices, for a selfish or evil end.

Magic circle: A circle drawn on the ground, or marked by pebbles, thorns, fire or water, around a person or object as protection from danger. When calling up spirits for consultation, the black magician usually stands inside a magic circle for safety.

Magic diagrams: Geometrical designs, meant to be symbolical representations of the mysteries of creation, the Deity and of the universe, and used for conjurations and evocations.

Magic drum: A wooden drum covered with reindeer skin, used by shamanistic magicians of the Eskimos and Laplanders for establishing rapport with the spirit world, for divinations, etc.

Magic herbs: Herbs considered to possess magic properties.

Magic mirror: Any shiny or light-reflecting surface used for *scrying* (q.v.).

Magic numbers: Certain numbers which are regarded as representing mysteries of the creation and divine secrets, and therefore considered to be possessing magic powers.

Magic ring: An amulet in the form of a ring worn by magicians, either to draw supernatural powers through them or as a sign of a bondage.

Magical works: See: *Seven magical works.*

Magician: A practitioner of the magic arts.

Magnetic mirror: A crystal globe filled with magnetized water, used for *scrying* (q.v.).

Magnetism: See: *Animal magnetism; od.*

Mahabharata: The ancient epic poem of India, of about 215,000 lines. It includes the *Bhagavad Gita*, the scripture in which Krishna appears.

Mahabhuta: In Hindu and occult philosophies, a physical element; in the Sankhya (q.v.) one of the five gross elements contrasted with the *Tanmatras* (q.v.).

Mahachohan: According to occult philosophy, an Elder Brother (q.v.), one of the three leaders of the Great White Lodge (q.v.); he is concerned, in some of his many incarnations, with the higher aspects of civilization and culture of the human race.

Maharshi: In Hindu mythology and occultism, Vishnu as the source of the paths to Realization. The term is applied also to great sages who disclose new paths to Realization.

Mahasamadhi: In Hindu mystic terminology, the ultimate absorption in the Spirit.

Mahat: Short for *mahatattva*, meaning in Sanskrit *great principle*. The Cosmic Intelligence, the first motion that arises in the supreme ideal universe, the first departure from the original condition, the first product of the Cosmic Substance (*prakriti*).

Mahatma: Sanskrit for *great soul*. An adept of occult sciences and arts who has attained the highest degree of esoteric knowledge. In theosophical terminology, the name is applied to a class of great ones, "elder brothers," "masters of wisdom and compassion," living in India and Tibet, who, because of their sympathy for mankind, have renounced the privilege of continuing further their spiritual evolution, to help others who are less advanced than they themselves.

Mahatattva: See: *Mahat*.

Mahavairocana: The Buddha of the Mystical School "who illumines the whole world as the sun does." The universe is his Lawbody (see *trikaya*) forever propagating his truth, and all phenomena are his manifestations.

Mahayana Buddhism: "Great Vehicle Buddhism," the Northern, Sanskrit, Tibetan, and Chinese form of Buddhism (q.v.), extending as far as Korea and Japan, whose central theme is that Buddhahood means devotion to the salvation of others and thus manifests itself in the worship of Buddha and Bodhisattvas (q.v.). Apart from absorbing beliefs of a more primitive strain, it has also evolved metaphysical and epistemological systems, such as the Sunya-vada (q.v.) and Vijnana-vada (q.v.).

Mahayuga: Sanskrit for *great age;* the *manvantara* (q.v.).

Mahdi: An Arabic word, literally meaning *the guided one*. The future leader of the Mohammedans who is to appear as a Messiah, to establish the better age.

Major arcana: The 22 tarot cards of the *tarot* (q.v.) deck.

Makom: A Hebrew mystical designation of God, as the One in whom everything that is existing exists.

Male principle; masculine force: In esoteric philosophy, the active and positive aspect of cosmic order or force or of the deity. The male principles are represented by male gods in the pantheons of polytheistic religions.

Malefic: A term applied in astrology to certain planets deemed to exert a harmful influence; chiefly Mars and Saturn. As usually employed, it is loosely applied to an inharmonious aspect with any planet, and to a conjunction with any malefic planet.

Malevolence: Ill or evil will or disposition—the will or disposition to do wrong or to harm others. The opposite of benevolence or good will.

Malleus maleficarum: The title of the treatise of Henry Kramer and James Sprenger (published in 1489) describing the manifestations of witchcraft and prescribing appropriate answers for those who doubted the existence of devils and demons.

Malphas: In demonography, a high-ranking demon ("grand president") of the infernal empire.

Mamaloi: A West Indian voodoo priestess-magician.

Mana: A power or influence believed to be inherent in or pertaining to objects or forces in non-human nature and to the dead; a potency which spirits of nature and ghosts of the dead have and can convey, and which may act from spirits through objects and forces. The word is of Melanesian origin.

Manang: The shamanistic medicine-man of the aborigines of Borneo.

Manas: Sanskrit for *mind* or *mentality*. The reasoning faculty, intelligence, understanding, the individual mind, the power of attention, selection and rejection.

Mandragora: In occult lore, a familiar demon. Mandragoras are believed to appear to mortal eyes as small, beardless men.

Manes: In Roman mythology, the souls of the dead, residing in the nether world; they were worshipped with offerings of food and drink at the graves.

Manicheism: A mystical religio-philosophical doctrine, instituted in Persia by Mani (Manes or Manichaeus), a Magian who, upon conversion to Christianity, sought to synthesize the latter with the dualism of Zoroastrianism, and became a martyr to his faith. The Manicheist creed teaches that to combat the powers of darkness, the mother of light created the first man. As Buddha and Zoroaster, he worked illumination among men; as Jesus, the Son of Man, he had to suffer, become transfigured and symbolize salvation by his apparent death at the cross; as spirit of the sun he attracts all connatural light particles to himself. But final salvation from the throes of evil demons is accomplished by ascetic living, reminding of the Hindu code of ethics, and belief in Mani as the prophesied paraclete.

Manitou: An American Indian (Algonquin) word for a force inherent in matter, felt as an expression of spirit; any sort of spirit, found mostly in non-human objects.

Mansions of the Moon: In astrology, a series of 28 divisions of the Moon's travel through one complete circuit of 360 degrees, each Mansion representing one day's average travel of the moon (12°51'25.2", or roughly 13 degrees), beginning apparently at the point of the Spring Equinox, or 0° Aries.

Mantic: Relating to or capable of divination and seer-craft.

Mantic frenzy: A state of ecstasis or semi-trance.

Mantra: A Sanskrit term meaning an incantation consisting of a sacred formula, usually a quotation from the Vedas. The word has come, especially in occult usage, to mean a spell or charm. In Shaktism and elsewhere, the holy syllables to which, as manifestations of the eternal word or sound, great mystic significance and power is ascribed.

Mantra yoga: That school of Yoga which seeks union with the divine spirit by working not only on the etheric plane (cf. *laya yoga*) but reaching to the anterior places of creative sentiment and ideas. Recitation of prayers and praises of the Deity is the essential part of *mantra yoga*.

Mantradhyana: A Sanskrit term for spiritual awareness produced or reinforced by incantations.

Mantram: The same as *mantra* (q.v.).

Manu: A Sanskrit name for the progenitor of the human race; also, any person regarded as the potential archetype for his fellowmen. In occult philosophy, an Elder Brother (q.v.), one of the three leaders of the Great White Lodge (q.v.), who, in his various incarnations at various periods of history, is the head of each root race (q.v.) and directs its racial characteristics and evolution.

Manvantara: Sanskrit for *cycle* in cosmic history. The current *manvantara* of Hindu mystic philosophy embraces the *Satya Yuga*, the *Golden Age* (the first four-tenths of the cycle), followed by the *Dwapara Yuga*, the *Second Age* (three-tenths of the cycle), the *Tretya Yuga*, the *Third Age* (two-tenths of the cycle), and the current *Kali Yuga*, the *Dark Age* (one-tenth of the duration of the entire cycle), in which we are living now.

Marchocias: In demonography, a high-ranking demon of the infernal empire, honest and loyal to the magician who invokes him.

Marduk: In Babylonian mythology, the king of all the gods, determiner of destiny, god of magicians and magic arts.

Marga: Sanskrit for *path;* used in the sense of method or approach in the endeavor to attain spiritual enlightenment. (See *bhakti-marga, jnana-marga, karma-marga.*)

Margaritomancy: Divination by interpreting the relative positions of pearls thrown on a flat surface.

Mars: Originally a Roman god of agriculture, later the god of war, identified with the Greek Ares.

Marthim: A demon, ranking high in the infernal empire. (Also called *Bathym.*)

Martinists: An occult society founded in France by Louis Claude de Saint-Martin in the later part of the 18th century. Originally, it was an occult Masonic society following the "rectified rite" originated by Saint-Martin, which emphasized occultism, theurgy and the communication with planetary spirits and other discarnate intelligences.

Maru: See: *Meru.*

Masculine force: See: *Male principle.*

Mason, Masonry: See: *Freemason, Freemasonry.*

Master: A higher initiate; a teacher. A degree in many occult cults and esoteric societies. Frequently used in occultism also as a synonym for Mahatma or Elder Brother (q.v.).

Master mason: In Freemasonry, a person who has been awarded the third degree of initiation.

Master of wisdom: A designation, used especially in literature of the Theosophical Society, for an Elder Brother (q.v.).

Master of wisdom and compassion: See: *Mahatma.*

Materia prima: See: *Prime matter.*

Materialism: A proposition that only matter is existent or real; that matter is the primordial or fundamental constituent of the universe; that only sensible entities, processes, or content are existent or real; that the universe is not governed by intelligence, purpose, or final causes; that everything is strictly caused by material (inanimate, non-mental, or having certain elementary physical powers) processes or entities (mechanism); that mental entities, processes, or events (though existent) are caused solely by material entities, processes, or events and themselves have no causal effect (*epiphenomenalism*); that nothing supernatural exists (naturalism); that nothing mental exists; that everything is explainable in terms of matter in motion or matter and energy or simply matter (depending upon the conception of matter entertained); that the only objects science can investigate are the physical or material (that is, public, manipulable, non-mental, natural, or sensible). Materialism denies the truth of all doctrines and beliefs of occultism, metaphysics, esoteric philosophy, etc.

Materialist: In esoteric terminology, a person who gives or ascribes material form and existence to that which is purely spiritual.

Materialization: In occult and especially spiritualist terminology, the assumption of material form. In spiritualism, the term is used for the appearance of spirits of the dead in material form, which is considered a temporary body formed of materials drawn from the atmosphere and from the emanations of the living beings present. Theosophists believe that these phenomena are produced by the Kama Rupa (q.v.) of the dead.

Materialization: In the terminology of scholasticism, the function of matter when it receives form and with it constitutes a body, as distinguished from *information* (q.v.).

Matrubhateswara: In Hindu religious mysticism and occultism, Ishwara (the Personal God) in the manifestation as the Mother.

Matter: The physical or non-mental; the physical, bodily, or non-spiritual; the relatively worthless or base; the worldly or natural (non-supernatural); the defining characteristics of which are extension, occupancy of space, mass, weight, motion, movability, inertia, resistance, impenetrability, attraction and repulsion, or their combinations; these characteristics or powers themselves; the extra-mental cause of sense experience; what composes the "sensible world"; the manipulable.

Maya: A Sanskrit term, approximately meaning *illusion*. In Hinduism and other occult and esoteric philosophies, the cosmic force which produces the phenomena of material existence and permits them to be perceived. All that is finite and subject to change and decay, all that is not eternal and unchangeable, is considered as *maya*. There is but one reality, Brahman-atman, the Universal Spirit.

Mazda: The name of two deities of ancient Persia. Prior to the sixth century B.C., Ahura Mazda was revered as a great personalized nature power; later, Mazda came to mean a cosmic power, whose nature is akin to all human and non-human spiritual beings and who rules all.

Mazdaism: A Persian religion, evolved in the fifth century B.C., centering about the chief cosmic deity, Mazda.

Meaning relation: See: *Name relation.*

Medical astrology: That branch of astrology which is concerned with the planetary causes of disease.

Medicine-man: The priest-magician of the American Indian tribes. Medicine-men were specialists in the techniques of healing, sorcery and divination, custodians of sacred objects, masters of ceremonial lore and magic. The word is often used for tribal priest-magicians of other races, where the proper designation would be witch-doctor or shaman.

Meditation school of Buddhism: See: *Zen Buddhism.*

Medium: A person who acts as an intermediary for communications between the material world and the spirit world; one capable of making contact with discarnate or other non-human entities.

Medium Cœli: See: *Midheaven.*

Mediumistic: An adjective meaning relating to, characteristic of or produced by a medium or mediums.

Mediumship: In spiritualism, the ability to communicate with beings on other planes of existence.

Medusa: The mortal one of the three Gorgons (q.v.) of Greek mythology. She was originally a beautiful maiden, but after she became the mother, by Poseidon, of Chrysaor and Pegasus, Athene (Minerva) changed her hair into hissing serpents, and everybody who looked at her was turned into stone. She was slain by Perseus.

Megacosm: The world of the astral light (q.v.), neither macrocosm (q.v.) nor microcosm (q.v.) but "something between the two."

Megaera: One of the three Furies (q.v.).

Melosinae: Undines (q.v.).

Memory of Nature: The *Akashic Records* (q.v.).

Mensambulism: Literally, *table-walking;* table-turning (q.v.).

Menstruum universale: The Latin name of the universal solvent (q.v.) sought by the alchemists.

Mental body: The "body" in which, according to occult philosophy, the conscious personality of man lives on the mental plane of existence, after "death" on the astral plane. Marc Edmund Jones calls it "the agency by which an individual functions in transcendental realms of idea, or through self-sufficient consciousness."

Mental chemistry: Psychological procedure, analogous to chemical analysis and synthesis, consisting in the attempted explanation of mental states as the products of the combination and fusion of psychic elements.

Mental plane; mental world: The plane of existence after the *astral plane;* the plane where man is believed by occultists to live in the *mental body* after "death" on the astral plane.

Mental word: In Latin, *verbum mentis;* the concept; the intramental product of the act of intellection.

Mentalism: Metaphysical theory of the exclusive reality of individual minds and their subjective states.

Mercury: The Roman god identified with the Greek Hermes (q.v.).

Mercury: In the terminology of medieval alchemists, the *quintessence* (q.v.).

Mercury of Nature: See: *Astral light.*

Mermaid; merman: Mythical creatures inhabiting the depths of the seas; their bodies are combination of human heads, arms and torsos and the tail of a fish. The male of the species is called *merman,* the female is called *mermaid.*

Meru: In Buddhist mythology and occult tradition, the mountain situated at the center of the earth; it is regarded as the spiritual center of the universe. (Also called *Maru.*)

Mesmerism: An obsolete name for *hypnotism* (q.v.).

Messiah; Messias: In Hebrew mysticism, the Savior who will come to restore the Chosen People to its rightful place in the world.

Metagnomy: A scientific term for knowledge obtained without the use of any of the five normally known human senses.

Metagraphology: *Psychometry* (q.v.) in which handwriting or a handwritten script serves as the basis of the divination.

Metaphysical dualism: The view that there are two realities—mind and matter, or God and the world-stuff.

Metaphysical naturalism: That view of reality which holds that reality is nature, and that the ultimate is found within the framework of nature.

Metaphysics: In general, the philosophical theory of reality. Defined variously as the rational science of the supernatural or supersensuous, the science of formal and final causes, the science of the obscure, occult or mysterious.

Metapsychics: A term coined by Prof. Richet and defined by him in his inaugural address as newly elected president of the Society for Psychical Research (in 1905), as "a science dealing with mechanical or psychological phenomena due to forces which seem to be intelligent, or to unknown powers, latent in human intelligence."

Metatron: According to the Hebrew Kabbalah, the angel who inhabits the Briatic world (see *Briah*), constituting the world of true spirit and governing the visible world.

Metempsychosis: The doctrine that the soul occupies another body after the death of the gross body. While the classical concept of metempsychosis includes the belief that the soul dwelling in a human may later occupy an animal body, too, occultists hold that the soul occupying a human body can be reincarnated in another human body only, and deny that the soul can migrate into a physical body on a lower scale of physical evolution.

Meteorological Astrology: See: *Astrometeorology*.

Miao: In Chinese mysticism, this word has two meanings: (a) Mystery of existence, which is unfathomable. (Lao Tzu.) (b) Subtlety, such as the subtle presence of the Omnipotent Creative Power (*shen*) in the myriad things.

Microcosm: Literally, *the small universe*—the term used by theosophists and occultists for man, regarded as a replica of the macrocosm (the *great universe*), because it contains all the elements, qualities and potencies of the latter.

Mictlan: The underworld which is the abode of the dead in Aztec mythology; it is ruled by Mictlantecuhtli, god of the dead, and his wife, Mictlancihuatl, goddess of death.

Midgard serpent: In Norse mythology, a great snake-like monster (*Midgardsormr*) which lies in the sea, coiled around the earth; one of the offspring of Loki. At the end of the world, the serpent will come out of the sea and join the attack of the other monsters and giants on the gods, and will kill Thor with its poisonous breath.

Midheaven: An astrological term applicable to the South point of the map, and what it indicates is dependent on the manner of interpretation employed. Sometimes loosely applied to the whole of the Tenth House. (Variously called Medium Cœli [M.C.], Southern angle, South point, and cusp of the Tenth House. Also improperly called the Zenith.)

Midrash: Hebrew for *interpretation* (plural: *Midrashim*). *Midrashim* are books interpreting the Holy Scriptures.

Mimamsa: Short for *Purva-Mimamsa*, one of the six major systems of Indian philosophy, founded by Jaimini, rationalizing Vedic ritual and upholding the authority of the Vedas by a philosophy of the word (see *vac*). In metaphysics it professes belief in the reality of the phenomenal, a plurality of eternal souls, but is indifferent to a concept of God though assenting to the superhuman and eternal nature of the Vedas. There is also an elaborate epistemology supporting Vedic truths, an ethics which makes observance of Vedic ritual and practice a condition of a good and blissful life.

Mimpathy: "Co-experiencing," not necessarily involving sympathy. The suffering of another must already be given in some form before it is possible for anyone to become a fellow sufferer. Pity and sympathy as experienced are always subsequent to the already apprehended and understood experience of another person who is pitied. One may share another's feeling about a matter, and yet have no sympathy for that one.

Mind: Generically considered, a metaphysical substance which pervades all individual minds and which is contrasted with matter or material substance. In occult philosophy, an immortal part of man's soul and personality, which uses the brain as a physical agent or vehicle for some of its functions.

Mind-dust theory: The theory that individual minds result from the combination of particles of mind which have always existed in association with material atoms. The rival theory is emergent evolution which assumes that mind is a novel emergent in the process of biological evolution.

Mind reading: The ability to be aware, or the awareness itself, of another person's thoughts without or even despite of his will. The term is often but improperly used for *telepathy* (q.v.) which properly used implies a two-way communication between two minds.

Mind-stuff theory: The theory that individual minds are constituted of psychic particles analogous to physical atoms. Differs from *mind-dust theory* (q.v.) in its emphasis on the constitution rather than the genesis of mind.

Ming: Chinese for *fate, destiny, decree of heaven.*

Ming te: A Chinese term for (a) Illustrious virtue; perfect virtue (Early Confucianism); (b) man's clear character; the virtuous nature which man derives from Heaven (Neo-Confucianism).

Minor arcana: The 56 suit cards of the *tarot* (q.v.) deck.

Miracle: An event contradictory to or inexplicable by known natural laws and teachings of exoteric science.

Mirific word: The hidden name of God, said to produce wonders when properly pronounced.

Mirror of the sorcerers: Any mirror or shiny or reflecting surface, also a vessel filled with water, used for *scrying* (q.v.).

Mishnah: Hebrew for *repetition;* the name of the older part of the *Talmud* (q.v.), containing Jewish laws and traditions from the close of the Old Testament till the end of the second century A.D., when it was compiled.

Mithraic mysteries: See: *Mithraism.*

Mithraism: A mystery cult or religion originating in Persia, very popular in the Roman Empire. Its hero-divinity, Mithra, devoted his life on earth to the service of mankind and was believed by his followers to have ascended to heaven and to continue to help the faithful in their fight against the forces of evil. The Mithraists had a very elaborate process of initiation, and the candidate had to pass through seven grades, symbolizing the passage of the soul after death through the seven heavens to the final dwelling place of the blessed. Mithraism restricted its membership to men.

Mixcoatl: An ancient Mexican god of war, thunder and hunting; according to the Aztec cosmology, one of the gods aiding in the creation of the world.

Moha: A Sanskrit term, meaning distraction, perplexity, delusion, beclouding of the mind, rendering it unfit to perceive the truth, generally explained as attachment to the phenomenal; in Buddhism, ignorance, as a source of vice.

Mohammedanism: The commonly applied term in the Occident to the religion founded by Mohammed. It sought to restore the indigenous monotheism of Arabia, Abraham's uncorrupted religion. Its essential dogma is the belief in the absolute unity of Allah. Its chief commandments are: profession of faith, ritual prayer, the payment of the alms tax, fasting and the pilgrimage. It has no real clerical caste, no church organization, no liturgy, and rejects monasticism. Its ascetic attitude is expressed in warnings against woman, in prohibition of nudity and of construction of splendid buildings except the house of worship; condemns economic speculation; praises manual labor and poverty; prohibits music, wine and pork, and the portrayal of living beings.

Mohanes: Shamanistic medicine-men of Peruvian Indians.

Moksha: In Hindu and occult terminology, the ultimate realization of identity with the Spirit. (Literally, *release* or *liberation*.) The identification of oneself with the ultimate reality, eternal, changeless, blissful, or in a state of complete indifference either with or without loss of consciousness, but at any rate beyond good and evil, pleasure and pain.

Moloch: A pagan Semitic deity, to whom children were sacrificed in fire.

Molybdomancy: Divination by interpreting the shapes formed by molten lead dropped on a flat surface.

Monad: In Greek philosophy, the Unit; originally, the number One, later any individual or metaphysical unit. Numerology still uses the term monad for the number One. According to Giordano Bruno, a metaphysical unit, a microscopic embodiment of the divine essence which pervades and constitutes the universe. Leibniz identified the monads with the metaphysical individuals or souls. In occult terminology, the monad is an indivisible divine spiritual life-atom, the immortal part of man which lives on in successive reincarnations.

Monergism: The view that the human will contributes nothing to its regeneration but that this is the work of one factor, the Divine.

Monition: The disclosure, usually with the connotation of a warning, of a past or contemporary occurrence without the agency of the five normal human senses. (Cf. *premonition.*)

Monotheism: The belief in only one God, the Creator and ruler of all things in the universe.

Monstrum: (Plural: *Monstra.*) In the literature of occultism and magic, an unnatural being, created by corruption or produced by unnatural sexual acts, the putrefaction of sperms or a morbid imagination.

Mortal mind: In Christian Science, "that self-contradictory consciousness with which the individual mortal man identifies himself, unless by education and religious craving for metaphysical completeness he recognizes its fallacious character. It has a certain resemblance to *Maya* (q.v.). Christian Science explains that mortal mind consciousness is an erroneous point of view, and asserts that all imperfection, evil, physical objectivity seen as matter, are misrepresentations of a metaphysically perfect universe. *Mortal mind* stands in opposition to the ethical nature of the metaphysical universe." (H. W. Steiger.)

Mortuary magic: Magic rites and practices aimed at assuring that a deceased person will have a pleasant life in the spirit world. This branch of magic became an elaborate art and science in ancient Egypt in particular.

Mother-goddess: A goddess appearing in every primitive religion or nature cult where the maintenance of fertility is a central interest; the representation of the deification of the female principle in the life and nature of the human race.

Mount Maru (Meru): See: *Meru.*

Mudra: The "mystic seal" of Oriental occultism; a series of occult signs made with the fingers, and considered to have magical effects.

Mukta: In Hindu mystic terminology, a person who has attained *Moksha* (q.v.).

Mukti: Sanskrit for *liberation*. The final release from worldly existence; final beatitude.

Multiple-colored sect of Lamaism: See: *Sakya*.

Multilocation: The phenomenon in which a body occupies or seems to be present in three or more places simultaneously. (Simultaneous presence in *two* places is called *bilocation*.)

Multiple personality: The apparent existence of two or more alternating personalities in the same individual, unknown to each other.

Mumia: In occultism, the essence of life contained in some physical vehicle, such as a severed part of a body, bodily excrements, secretions, etc.

Mummy: A human body embalmed and preserved according to the ancient Egyptian rites.

Mundane astrology: An interpretation of astrology in terms of world trends, the destinies of nations and of large groups of individuals, based on an analysis of the effects of equinoxes, solstices, new moons, eclipses, planetary conjunctions, and similar celestial phenomena; as distinguished from Natal Astrology, which is specifically applicable to an individual birth horoscope.

Mundane mind: In occult terminology, mind functioning on the material plane of existence, through the agency of the physical body and the physical brain, bent upon preserving these physical vehicles.

Muni: Sanskrit for *sage*. A seer, ascetic, monk, devotee.

Muses: Nine goddesses of Greek mythology, daughters of Zeus and Mnemosyne. Each muse presides over an art or science and inspires the poets or artists in their creative moments.

Music of the spheres: An expression introduced by Pythagoras, who was the first to discover a mathematical relationship in the frequencies of the various tones of the musical scale. In postulating the orbits of the planets as bearing a similar relationship based upon the distance from the center, he characterized their interrelated orbits as "the harmony of the spheres." According to G. A. Gaskell, the music of the spheres is "a symbol of the complete coordination and harmony that prevails among the atma-budhic qualities and ideals upon the higher planes or spheres of the invisible archetypal universe."

Mut: The ancient mother-goddess of Thebes (Egypt), representing the powers of the watery flood; she was worshipped as the wife of the Nile.

Mutable signs: A synonym for *double-bodied signs* (q.v.).

Mute signs: The astrological signs Cancer, Scorpio and Pisces; so named by the Arabian astrologers because they are symbolized by dumb creatures that emit no sounds.

Myomancy: Divination by observing rats or mice.

Mystagogue: An adept who acts as initiator into the esoteric mysteries.

Mysteries: In occultism or esoteric philosophies, this term is used in general for any occult discipline or body of teachings or practice, the nature and meaning of which cannot be divulged to non-initiates. Specifically, rites of antiquity in which priests, initiates and neophytes enacted allegorical scenes from the lives of gods and goddesses, the secret meaning of which was explained to new adherents upon initiation. (See *Dionysian mysteries; Eleusinian mysteries; Isis-Osiris mysteries; Mithraism; mystery cult; Orphic mysteries; Phrygian mysteries.*)

Mystery cult; mystery religion: This term is commonly employed to mean any religion or cult to which initiates are admitted by secret rites, the meaning of which cannot be divulged to the public; the possession of this esoteric knowledge is believed to insure special blessings for the devoted initiate both in earthly life and after physical death. The term is frequently used for the *mysteries* (q.v.) of classical Greece and Egypt although it is not very appropriate in this application, since these cults did not demand exclusive allegiance of the adherents and did not preclude their acceptance and observance of other gods and ritual practices.

Mystery language: According to H. P. Blavatsky (*The Key to Theosophy*), "The sacerdotal secret 'jargon' used by the initiated priests, and employed only when discussing sacred things. Every nation had its own 'mystery' tongue, unknown to all save those admitted to the Mysteries."

Mystes: The name given to initiates in the ancient mysteries (q.v.).

Mystic: While the original meaning of the word, as used in ancient times, was "initiated in the mysteries," the modern connotation is "one who believes in or practices mysticism."

Mystical night: The practice of the Sufis consisting in "disconnecting" all physical senses of perception, shutting out all external impressions and all emotions in order to induce a state of mystic contemplation and receptivity to inner enlightenment.

Mystical School of Buddhism: That school in Buddhist philosophy which considers the universe itself to be the Great Sun Buddha (*Mahavairocana*).

Mysticism: Any philosophy, doctrine, teaching or belief centered more on the worlds of the Spirit than the material universe, and aimed at the spiritual union or mental one-ness with the Universal Spirit, through intuitive and emotional apprehension of spiritual reality, and through various forms of spiritual contemplation, or disciplines. Mysticism in its simplest and most essential meaning is a type of religion which puts the emphasis on immediate awareness of relation with God, direct and intimate consciousness of Divine Presence. It is religion in its most acute, intense and living stage. The basic idea of all mysticism is that the essence of life and of the world is an all-embracing spiritual substance which is the true reality in the core of all beings, regardless of their outer appearances or activities.

Myth: A traditional story or legend of religious import, especially an account of the activities of supernatural entities. A presentation of cosmology, employing the affective method of symbolic representation in order to escape from the limitations of literal meaning.

Mythographer: A writer or recorder of myths.

Mythology: The organized body of the myths of peoples or races having a common tradition and inheritance. Also, the study of myths, their origin and nature.

N

Na Chia: In Taoism, the coordination and interlocking of the Ten Celestial Stems with the Eight Elements (*pa kua*), to the end that the first Stem, which is the embodiment of the active or male cosmic force, and the second Stem, which is the reservoir of the passive or female cosmic force, gather in the center and the highest point in the universe.

Nabi: In Hebrew mysticism, an interpreter of oracles, a messenger of the deity or spirit. The Nabis were not magicians, but seers.

Nadir: The lowest point below the Earth; the opposite point to the Zenith. It should not be confused with the Imum Cœli (q.v.).

Nagualism: A mystery cult of Mexico and Central America.

Naiad: In occultism, a nature-spirit or elemental of rivers, lakes and springs.

Nama-rupa: Sanskrit for *name (and) form*. The phenomenal world, or its conceptual and material aspects.

Name relation: The relation between a symbol (formula, word, phrase) and that which it denotes or of which it is the name.

Narcotic mirror: A round crystal globe filled with magnetized water in which a narcotic powder is dissolved; used for *scrying* (q.v.).

Nascent: A term applied to a thing or a state of mind at an early stage of its development when it is as yet scarcely recognizable. *Nascency* is the state of being nascent.

Nastrond: The frozen underworld, abode of the dead, in Nordic and Icelandic mythology.

Nasu: In Zoroastrian demonology, a female demon which feeds on the corpses of the dead and when forced to leave the corpse, leaves it in the shape of a fly.

Nat: In Burmese folklore, a nature-spirit of the forest.

Native: In astrological terminology, the subject of a celestial figure. (Cf. *Figure.*)

Nativity: In astrology: (1) The birth moment; the instant when the native drew his first breath, thereby commencing a process of blood conditioning that up to that moment had been accomplished through the receptivities of another. During the first days of life, in accordance with the law of adaptability, there ensues a growth of channels of receptivity to cosmic energy which results in a life-pattern of cosmic stimulation. (2) A Figure, or horoscope, cast for a date, moment and place of birth, as distinguished from an Electional or Horary Figure.

Natura naturans: God as the active power of nature. (A term introduced by Averroës, also used by Spinoza.)

Natura naturata: The world as the complex unity of individual things, the substance created by God, the *natura naturans*. (A term introduced by Averroës and used by Spinoza.)

Natural light: See: *Lumen naturale.*

Natural magic: The performance of supernatural acts through a more profound knowledge of natural phenomena.

Natural man: A term used by many occult philosophies to designate a human being who "is deceived by physical senses" and is therefore a prey to erroneous beliefs and not immune to physical disease of the flesh. (Cf. *spiritual man.*)

Natural omen: A sign of some future event drawn from the elements, animals or plants, and applying solely to events independent of human will.

Naturalism: The view, challenging the cogency of the cosmological, metaphysical, teleological, and moral arguments, which holds that the universe requires no supernatural cause and government, but is self-existent, self-explanatory, self-operating, and self-directing. (Cf. *metaphysical naturalism.*)

Nature: The general cosmic order, usually conceived as divinely ordained, in contrast to human deviations from this; that which exists apart from and uninfluenced by man.

Nature-spirit: An *elemental* (q.v.).

Nature worship: The expression of man's feeling of dependence on the powers of nature, of his gratitude to beneficent phases of his natural environment and of his fear of its dangerous elements. Almost all ancient gods were personified powers of nature.

Necessitarianism: The theory that every event in the universe is determined by logical or causal necessity. Necessitarianism, as a theory of cosmic necessity, becomes in its special application to the human will, *determinism* (q.v.).

Necromancy: Sorcery, witchcraft in general; specifically, the raising of images of the dead, and the practice of infusing life into the unconscious elementaries of the dead and using them for evil ends. Considered *Black Magic*.

Nectar: The drink of the gods of Greek mythology.

Nectromancy: The perception of the inner essence of things.

Necyomancy: Foretelling the future by examining the nerves of the dead.

Need-fire: Fire lit by turning a round piece of wood in a hole bored in another piece of wood; believed to have supernatural properties, especially the power to protect or cure from pestilence any animal driven through it. All fires in the vicinity must be extinguished while the need-fire is being kindled, and after the animals have been driven through it, the family fire is relit from the need-fire.

Negative hallucination: The failure to perceive an object which is in fact present to the organs of sense. (Cf. *Hallucination*.)

Nei sheng: A Chinese term used in referring to the man who attained to complete self-cultivation, sagehood. (Confucius.)

Nei tan: The Chinese term for "internal alchemy," the deification of man's spirit.

Nembutsu: In Japanese Buddhism, "thinking of Buddha," the process of repeating the name of Buddha and meditating on him.

Nemesis: In Greek mythology, the goddess, daughter of the Night, who pursues and punishes the haughty and the criminal.

Nenufaremi: In occult lore, a name for elementals (q.v.) of the air.

Neophyte: A novice in occult or esoteric discipline. A candidate for initiation into the mysteries.

Neo-Platonism: The mystic philosophical system established by

Plotinus (205-270 A.D.). Its center is the Godhead, the One, the Absolute Good, the Source, an undivided and undifferentiated Unity, from which a succession of emanations radiate out in stages of decreasing splendor and reality.

Nephelomancy: Foretelling the future by using the clouds as divinatory signs.

Nephesh: Hebrew for *soul.* In Kabalistic terminology, the animal soul in man.

Nephilim: The Hebrew name of the giants of primeval times, regarded as fallen angels.

Neptune: An ancient Italian water deity, later identified in Roman mythology with the Greek god Poseidon, god of the sea.

Nereid: A sea nymph (q.v.) as opposed to the *naiads,* the nymphs of sweet waters.

Nergal: In Babylonian mythology, the god and ruler of the underworld where the spirits of the dead dwell.

Neshamah: The Kabalistic name of the divine soul in man.

Neutralism: The view that reality is neither mind nor matter but a single kind of stuff, of which mind and matter are but appearances or aspects.

New Thought: The name of a movement, based on the work of Phineas P. Quimby (1802-1866), who practiced mental and spiritual healing. The movement adopted the name *The National New Thought Alliance* in 1908, and became the *International New Thought Alliance* in 1914. Its constitution, adopted in 1916, states that its purpose is "to teach the Infinitude of the Supreme One, the Divinity of Man and his Infinite possibilities through the creative power of constructive thinking and obedience to the voice of the Indwelling Presence which is our source of Inspiration, Power, Health and Prosperity."

Nibbana: The Pali version of the term *nirvana* (q.v.).

Nimesha: A Sanskrit word for "extinction of the universe," synonymous with *pralaya* (q.v.).

Nine Jewels: In occult terminology, the culminating stage of spiritual development.

Ningma: The ancient, unreformed form of Lamaism (Tibetan Buddhism); called the Red Sect, rich in esoteric teachings and traditions.

Ninurta: In Babylonian and Assyrian mythology, the god of war and of storms, patron of physicians.

Nirguna: Sanskrit for "devoid of qualities" (*guna*), predicated as early as the Upanishads (q.v.) of the Absolute as its in-itself aspect (cf. *saguna*). The highest reality is conceived to be of such fullness, such transcendence that it has no part in the manifold of the phenomenal which is mere *maya* (q.v.) in Sankara's philosophy in so far as it is esoteric.

Nirguna Brahman: In the teachings of Yoga, God anterior to existence and without attributes, the higher aspect of the Deity, the mysterious source out of which the creatively active aspect Saguna Brahman (q.v.) emerges.

Nirvana: In the Oriental philosophical doctrines, the absolute and final extinction of individuality, without loss of consciousness. In occult and esoteric philosophical terminology, the ultimate absolute existence and consciousness attained by the Ego of one who in his life achieved supreme perfection and holiness. It is defined as a condition in which all pain, suffering, mental anguish and, above all, *samsara* (q.v.) have ceased.

Nirvanee: He who has attained Nirvana (q.v.).

Nitya-vada: The Vedantic (see *Veda*) theory (*vada*) which asserts that reality is eternal (*nitya*), change being unreal.

Nivashi: In the magic lore of the Gypsies of Southeastern Europe, a malignant water-spirit.

Nix; nixie: A nature-spirit of the water; a nymph.

Niyama: Sanskrit for *restraint* or *self-culture;* the second prerequisite in the study and practice of Yoga. The classic text *Hathayogapradipika* lists ten rules of inner control (*niyamas*), viz., penance, contentment, belief in God, charity, adoration of God, hearing discourses on the principles of religion, modesty, intellect, meditation, and sacrifice. (Cf. *yama.*)

Noble Truths: See: *Four Noble Truths.*

Nodes of the planets: The points at which the orbits of the planets intersect the ecliptic, because of the inclination of their planes to the plane of the Earth's orbit. One astrological authority states that a lunation or eclipse on the South Node of a planet tends to release a destructive force of the nature of the planet involved.

Norito: Japanese prayers recited by Shinto priests in religious ceremonies, and high state officials in state ceremonies. These stately, dignified prayers, standardized in form, give thanks to Shinto deities, invoke their blessings, and are believed to have magical effect.

Norns: Urd, Verdandi and Skuld, the equivalents in Norse mythology of the Roman Fates (q.v.).

Notes of the gamut: Having to do with what Pythagoras termed "the music of the spheres" (q.v.). C, The Sun; D, Saturn; E, Mercury; F, The Moon; G, Mars; A, Venus; B, Jupiter. Peculiarly, the next two planets discovered have, according to Sepharial, an axial rotation from east to west, contrary to the order of the other bodies. It is in reference to the Gamut that Uranus, Neptune and Pluto are spoken of as belonging to the second octave; Uranus, the octave of Mercury; Neptune, of Venus; and Pluto, of Mars.

Nous: In Neo-Platonism, theosophy and other occult doctrines, the Mind or Spirit, the first and most sublime stage of the emanations which issue forth from the Godhead, the Absolute Good, as light emanates from a luminous body. The Divine Mind in man. It is defined in the Rosicrucian Manual as "that energy, power and force emanating from the Source of all Life, possessing positive and negative polarity, manifesting it in vibrations of various rates of speed which, under certain conditions and obeying the dictates of natural law, establish the world of form, be that form visible or invisible."

Nox: In Roman mythology, the goddess personifying the night; daughter of Chaos, mother of the Day and the Light, of Dreams and Death.

Numen: In the religion of the Romans of antiquity, a divine power or spirit, whose presence was felt as an occult power.

Numerology: The study of the occult and magical properties of numbers. Each number is assigned a root meaning and diversified representations.

Nusku: The Assyrian god of fire.

Nyingpo: The Tibetan name of the World Soul (q.v.).

Nymph; nympha: In occultism, little, graceful, gay female nature-spirits, usually friendly; they are generally regarded as water-spirits (see *naiad, nereid, oceanid*), but some authors place the *dryads and hamadryads* (q.v.) in this class, too. Nymphs are regarded as long-lived, but not immortal, and possessing certain magical abilities.

Oahspe: "A new Bible in the Words of Jehovih and His Angel Ambassadors. A Sacred History of the Dominions of the Higher and Lower Heavens on the Earth for the past Twenty-four Thousand Years." A book published originally by the Essenes of Kosmon, a Fraternity of Faithists, and currently by Wing Anderson (Kosmon Industries, Los Angeles, Calif.) The preface to the eleventh American edition (copyright 1953 by E. Wing Anderson) states that OAHSPE (pronounced O as in *clock*, AH as in *father*, SPE as in *Speak*) means sky, earth and spirit and is the title of a new bible given to the world in the year 1881; it goes on to say that the book was written down, under spiritual guidance, by Dr. John B. Newbrough, who was gifted with astonishing extrasensory perception and was actively engaged in psychic research. The preface goes on to say that "OAHSPE purports to have been written at the command of God, who states that He is not the Creator but is simply chief executive officer . . . of our planet earth. He explains who the Creator is and also makes clear the difference between Lord, Lord God, God and the Creator. This strange book informs us that the world entered a new era in the year 1848, how the new era is different from those which preceded it and what changes will come to humanity within the next few years. . . . OAHSPE is made up of thirty-six books covering the history of the planet, the history of the human race, the history of every major religion, past and present, an analysis of today and a prophecy of tomorrow."

Ob: In Hebrew mysticism and occultism, the Spirit of Ob personifies the evil aspects of the astral light (q.v.).

Obaoba: A Polynesian medicine-man.

Obeah: A black magical cult of the West Indies.

Oberon: The king of the elementals of the air in English folklore.

Objective mind: The *mundane mind* (q.v.).

Obscuration: A theosophical term, originated by A. P. Sinnett, for the state of dormancy or latency of life-energies.

Obsession: In occult terminology, the control of a living person by a discarnate spirit which suppresses the normal personality of the person obsessed.

Occult: Hidden from the uninitiated. A synonym for *esoteric*. In every-day parlance, the word has come to mean supernatural, transcending the laws of the material world.

Occultation: The term applied by astrologers to the condition when a planet or star is hidden or eclipsed by another body, particularly by the Moon.

Occultism: Belief in hidden, mysterious, superhuman powers and the possibility of using or controlling them. Also, a synonym for *Occult Sciences* (q.v.).

Occult Sciences: In occult terminology, the science of living, the science of the secrets of nature which deals with things and concepts transcending material and sensual perception, expounding the brotherhood of sentient beings. Also called *Esoteric Sciences* or *Hermetic Sciences*.

Occultist: A student, adept or practitioner of occultism or the occult sciences.

Occursion: A general term applied by astrologers to celestial occurrences; such as, ingresses, formation of aspects, and conjunctions.

Occursor: A term applied by Ptolemy to the planet which moves to produce an occursion. In modern astrology, generally superseded by *Promittor*.

Oceanids: A nature-spirit or elemental (q.v.) of the class of nymphs, dwelling in the ocean. In Greek mythology, the oceanids were the 4,000 daughters of Okeanos and Tethys.

Och: The Olympian Spirit (q.v.), governing the Sun, ruler of 28 Olympian Provinces of the Universe; his day is Sunday.

Octad: In numerology, the number Eight.

Od: A name introduced (with its synonyms, *odic force, odyle,*

odyllic force) by Baron v. Reichenbach for a force or energy
which he discovered to emanate from crystals and magnets in the
dark. He described it as a force existing and emanating from every
object or substance, including the stars and planets, human and
animal bodies as well, transferable by contact and perceptible to
sensitives as an "odic flame" or "odic light.". The od and its effects
have been cited as the explanation of many mediumistic phenomena.

Odherir: The magic cauldron of the Norse myths.

Odic force: See: *Od.*

Odin: One of the Norse triad of deities (the other two were
Thor and Freyr); the god of war, the lord of the Valhalla (Hall
of the Chosen Dead). Later revered also as the creator of the
world and king of all gods.

Odyle; odyllic force: See: *Od.*

Oenomancy: Divination by interpreting the appearance of wine.

Oera Linda Boek: A Frisian manuscript which is claimed to
record a great deal of esoteric facts.

Ogam (Ogham) writing: A pre-Christian Celtic "writing"
found on numerous stone monuments in Ireland, Scotland and
Wales, using an alphabet of twenty letters, each letter consisting
of one to five lines or strokes in a certain position. It has been
suggested that this writing was invented by the Druids who used
it for secret signalling and as magical diagrams. (According to
Celtic legends, it was devised by the mythical Celtic chief Ogma.)
According to theosophists, Ogam was an early Celtic mystery
language (q.v.) and the Druids used the Ogam writing to record
messages written in this Ogam language.

Ogdoad: See: Octad.

Ogre: In occult lore, and in the folklore of certain races, an evil
nature-spirit of hideous appearance, at times a man-eating giant.

Oharai; ohoharahi: Literally, *great expulsion.* The Japanese
ritual of purification.

Olympian province: See: *Olympian Spirits.*

Olympian Spirits: According to the Arbatel, a magic ritual published in the late 16th century, spirits who dwell in the air and in
interplanetary space, each governing a certain number of the 196
Olympic Provinces into which the universe is divided. The seven
Olympic Spirits, also referred to as Stewards of Heaven, are:

Aratron, Bethor, Phaleg, Och, Hagith, Ophiel, and Phul (q.v.).

Olympus: A mountain in southern Thessaly; its perpetually cloud-capped peak (9,794 feet high) was believed to be the abode of the gods of the Greek-Roman pantheon.

Om: A Sanskrit word, variously interpreted and explained, believed to possess magical powers and held especially sacred by Hindus and occultists.

Om madri muye sale-hdu: The *mantra* (q.v.) used by the Bonists of Tibet instead of the Lamaist *om mani padme hum.*

Om mani padme hum: The most famous *mantra* (q.v.) of Lamaism.

Omen: An event or object believed to be a sign or token portending or foretelling the evil or beneficent character of a future occurrence.

Omnipotence: Absolute, perfect, unlimited power over all things.

Omnipresence: Power or property (of a deity) of being at all places and in all things.

Omniscience: In philosophy and theology it means the complete and perfect knowledge of God, of Himself and of all other beings, past, present, and future, or merely possible, as well as all their activities, real or possible, including the future free actions of human beings. (The adjective is: *omniscient.*)

Omniverse: A newly coined term for all creation in all space, as distinguished from "universe." The term "universe" should embrace the whole of the galaxy, and "omniverse" the galaxy of galaxies that embraces all known and unknown stars and star-clusters.

One-factor religion: A term coined by F. L. Parrish, to designate any religion in which religious ideas and practices are based on the doctrine of the unity of nature, and on the assumption that there is a common denominator through which the world order operates, a common natural bond which links man's nature with the nature of non-human objects, powers and forces.

Onirocritics: See: *Oniromancy.*

Oniromancy: The study of dreams (*oniroscopy*) and their interpretation (*onirocritics*).

Oniroscopy: See: *Oniromancy*.

Onomancy: Divination by interpreting the letters in a person's name.

Ontology: The theory of being as being. For Aristotle, the First Philosophy, the science of the essence of things. The science of fundamental principles; the doctrine of the categories. Ultimate philosophy; rational cosmology. Synonymous with *metaphysics*.

Onychomancy: Divination by observing nails exposed to the sunlight.

Oomancy; ooscopy: Divination by eggs.

Operative Masonry: That period of the history of Freemasonry when Masons actually worked in the building crafts as an occupation and source of livelihood.

Ophiel: The Olympian Spirit (q.v.) governing Mercury, ruler of 14 Olympian Provinces of the universe; his day is Wednesday.

Ophites: A Gnostic sect originating in Syria, which regarded the serpent as the symbol of the supreme emanation of the Godhead.

Oracle: In antiquity, an oracle was a temple or shrine where a god would speak to his worshippers through his priest or priestess; also, the priest or priestess through whose mouth the god speaks. In modern terminology, a medium who transmits messages from dwellers on other planes of existence; also, any such message received or transmitted by a medium or through other occult agencies.

Orbs: The term employed in astrology to describe the arc between the point at which a platic, or wide aspect, is deemed strong enough to be operative, and the point of culmination of a partile or exact aspect; the space within which an aspect is judged to be effective.

Ordeal: A method for determining the innocence or guilt of a suspect by subjecting him to painful or dangerous tests, supposedly under superhuman control.

Oread: A nature-spirit of the mountains.

Orenda: An American Indian (Iroquois) term for an inherent power or energy possessed and exerted, in some characteristic manner, by objects.

Ormuzd: Modern Persian version of the name Ahura Mazda (q.v.).

Ornithomancy: Divination using the song or flight of birds as divinatory signs.

Orobas: In demonography, a prince of the infernal empire, helpful and loyal to the magician who invokes him.

Orphic: Relating to or originating from the Orphic mysteries; a member of the Orphic mystery cult.

Orphic mysteries: The ancient Greek mystery cult which developed from the Dionysian mysteries (q.v.). The Orphics eliminated the orgiastic elements of the Dionysian rites, and invested their mysteries with a more sober and speculative character, emphasizing the immortality of the soul and the doctrine of reincarnation, the "Great Circle of Necessity." They taught a symbolism in which, for instance, the relationship of the One to the many was clearly enunciated, and they sought to influence their destiny after death by austerity and pure living.

Osiris: The most widely worshipped god of ancient Egypt, god of the dead, husband of Isis, father of Horus. He was worshipped also as the great Creator. His cult included human sacrifices, for which in later periods animal sacrifices were permitted to be substituted. His death and resurrection was the central theme of the Isis-Osiris mysteries.

Oudad: In numerology, the Zero.

Ouija board: An instrument for communication with the spirits of the dead. Made in various shapes and designs, some of them used in the sixth century before Christ. The common feature of all its varieties is that an object moves under the hand of the medium, and one of its corners, or a pointer attached to it, spells out messages by successively pointing to letters of the alphabet marked on a board which is a part of the instrument.

Ouroboros: A serpent biting its own tail, forming a circle; the symbol of the endless succession of incarnations which form the wheel of life.

Ousia: Greek for *substance* or *essence;* that Being which really *is* and remains, in contrast to the changing, ephemeral particulars of worldly phenomena.

Over-Mind: The *Nous* (q.v.).

Oversoul: This term is applied in occult philosophy as a synonym for *Brahma*, also as a synonym for *group soul* (q.v.), and as a name for the Absolute in its aspect of the reality which maintains all existence.

P

Pa kua: The Chinese name of the Eight Trigrams or Elements (Heaven, Earth, Thunder, Mountain, Fire, Water, Water in Motion, Wind and Wood); Chinese occultists attribute mystic and magical powers to these eight signs or their proper combinations. A figure consisting of the eight trigrams and used as a charm or an object of worship, is also called *pa kua*.

Palingenesy: Greek for *re-birth*. The transmigration of the life-energy or soul, retaining its identity, in recurrent cycles or phases. The term was employed by the occult philosophers of the seventeenth century to denote the "resurrection of plants," and the method of achieving their astral appearance after destruction. (L. Spence, An Encyclopaedia of Occultism.)

Palmistry: Divination through analysis of the lines, shapes, etc. of the hands. (Cf. *chirognomy, chiromancy, chirosophy.*)

Pan: The Arcadian god of shepherds, hunters and rural residents, chief of the minor deities of the Greek pantheon. Represented as a horned, long-eared man with the lower half of the body and legs resembling those of a goat; he plays a pipe on which he can produce music of magic power which "can charm the very gods."

Pandit: A Hindu term for *learned man*. (Often, wrongly, written *pundit*.)

Panentheism: The doctrine that all things are within the being of God, who is yet not merely the whole of actual things.

Panpsychism: The doctrine that the entire universe is animated.

Pan-Satanism: The vague belief that the world is somehow identified with the devil. This name was given by Herbart to pantheism.

Pantheism: The doctrine that reality comprises a single being of which all things are modes, moments, members, appearances, or projections. Pantheism teaches the essential immanence of God in all creatures and things, identifies God with Nature and Nature with God, teaching that the forces and laws manifest in the universe, the entire Cosmos, the whole of reality itself, *are* God.

Pantheistic personalism: The doctrine that reality consists of a Supreme Personality, of which the world of persons are parts. The Divine Personality having no separate existence from its creation.

Pantheon: The collective name of all the gods of a tribe, race or nation. Also, a temple dedicated to all the gods.

Papaloi: A West Indian voodoo priest-magician.

Paraaatman: A Sanskrit term for the Supreme or Universal Spirit.

Para handatar; para handandatar: A Hittite term for a special force through which the gods govern, individual to each god.

Parabrahm: Sanskrit for *beyond Brahma*. The impersonal, absolute, supreme Principle.

Paraclete: One who is called to assistance; one who brings succor. Usually, a divine saviour or redeemer.

Paramahamsa: A Sanskrit word, denoting a high adept or master of esoteric science, or an ascetic who has subdued all his physical senses by abstract meditation.

Parinama-vada: A theory of evolution expounded by the Sankhya (q.v.), according to which the disturbed equilibrium between two primary substances (*prakriti and purusha*) is responsible for change.

Paranirvana: Sanskrit for *beyond Nirvana*. The ultimate Nirvana (q.v.) of the Vedantic philosophers. In occult philosophy, absolute non-being, yet equivalent to absolute *sat* (q.v.).

Paranormal: A term used in parapsychology for the *supernatural.*

Parapsychic: An obsolescent term for *parapsychological* (q.v.). Its German equivalent, *parapsychisch*, is still in general use in the German-speaking countries.

Parapsychology: The study of supernormal abilities and phenomena. Defined in *The Journal of Parapsychology* as "a division of psychology dealing with those psychical effects which appear not to fall within the scope of what is at present recognized law."

Parasite: Any being or entity which lives on the physical or spiritual energy of another organism.

Parcae: See: *Fates.*

Paroptic sense: The faculty, claimed by many occultists to be attainable, of "seeing" with the *etheric body*, instead of or without using the eyes.

Parsi; Parsee: An Indian follower of Zoroastrianism.

Parsiism: The Indian branch of Zoroastrianism.

Parvati: A gentle and beautiful goddess of Shaivism, one of the consorts of Shiva.

Password: Any word known to the initiates or members of a group or society which assures admittance to meetings, rituals, etc.

Peach: In Chinese occult symbology, a symbol of longevity. (Cf. *fu lu shou.*)

Pegomancy: Divination using the water of a fountain for source of divinatory omens.

Penates: In Roman mythology, household spirits, spirits of the pantry; usually associated and invoked together with the *Lares* (spirits of the fields).

Pentad: In numerology, the number Five.

Pentagram: A magical diagram, consisting of a five-pointed star, representing Man; it is considered by occultists to be the most potent means of conjuring spirits. When a single point of the star points upward, it is regarded as the sign of the good and a means to conjure benevolent spirits; when the single point points down and a pair of points are on top, it is a sign of the evil (Satan) and is used to conjure powers of evil.

Perfect Land: In ancient Egyptian nomenclature, the plane of existence where the true or spirit forms of all things created exist —the *astral world* or *astral plane.*

Peri: In Persian mythology, a fairy-like creature descended from a race of fallen angels.

Periapt: An amulet or a charm worn to prevent disease or to ward off evil.

Persephone: In Greek mythology, daughter of the goddess Demeter; abducted by Hades to become his wife and queen of the underworld, she was allowed by Zeus to return to her mother for eight months in each year.

Personality: In esoteric philosophy, the mortal, personal Ego of man.

Personation: In psychical research and occultism, the temporary assumption of the physical and mental characteristics of other persons, with or without loss of one's consciousness and of the awareness of one's own true personal identity.

Pert em hru: The Egyptian *Book of the Dead* (q.v.).

Phaleg: The Olympian Spirit (q.v.) governing Mars, ruler of 35 Olympian Provinces of the universe; his day is Tuesday.

Phallic worship: See: *Phallism.*

Phallism: The worship of the generative or reproductive powers of nature symbolized by the sex organs. (Also called *phallicism* or *phallic worship.*)

Phantasmata: In occult terminology, spirits or thought-forms created by man's imagination and said to be able to communicate with him.

Phenomenal world: The world of appearance as opposed to the world as-it-is-in-itself.

Phenomenon (plural: *phenomena*). Any item of experience or reality. Kant divides the latter into: the *noumenon*, the thing in itself, which is utterly unknowable; and the *phenomenon*, which is the object of experience. In occult terminology applied to a cosmical chemical, or psychical impulse, experienced by one who is attuned to Nature's more sensitive forces. (In astrology, the term is applied to supplementary data in the ephemeris indicating the exact times of eclipses, of the passing of the Nodes and other points in the orbit, of conjunctions, of the lunar ingresses, and similar details.)

Philosopher's egg: In alchemical terminology, the vessel or container in which the final stage of the process of the transmutation of metals was performed.

Philosopher's stone: An imaginary substance by means of which the ancient alchemists sought to transmit baser metals into gold. Probably an early concept of a catalytic agent. Used in occult terminology to indicate the power by which all life evolves and through which all minds and souls realize a mutual kinship; it signifies the highest aspirations and the purest ideologies of altruism, and is a symbol of transmutation of lower animal nature into the superior divine one; the knowledge capable of solving all problems in life.

Philosophy: Literally, the love for and the pursuit of knowledge, and its application to daily affairs; in actual usage the knowledge of phenomena as explained by and resolved into reasons and causes, sources and forces and the laws applicable thereto.

Philtre: Any mystic or magical potion regarded capable of producing certain sentiments in the person who drinks it.

Phoenix: The mythical bird which is periodically destroyed by fire and rises to new life from the ashes.

Phone-voyance: A special form of clairvoyance, discovered and described by V. N. Turvey in 1905: the sensitive can "see" and describe objects and happenings in the physical vicinity of a person with whom he is talking over a telephone, including astral forms or spirits near the latter.

Phrygian mysteries: The mysteries or esoteric rites widely observed around the Mediterranean, centered around the mother-goddess Cybele who mourned the death of the youthful male deity Attis until he returned to life in the springtime.

Phul: The Olympian Spirit (q.v.) governing the Moon, ruler of seven Olympian Provinces of the universe; his day is Monday.

Physical body: The material, perishable, gross body which is destroyed at death.

Piai: A medicine-man or shamanistic medium of certain South American Indian tribes.

Ping t'ien hsia: World peace, the ultimate goal of Confucian moral training and education.

Pir: A teacher or guide in the mystical pursuit of Islam. In India, the Moslem equivalent of a Hindu *guru.*

Pisacha: The name given in India to vampirical *eidolons* (cf. *Kama Rupa*).

Piscean Epoch: The era of 2,000 years which, according to occult teachings, preceded the current "Aquarian Epoch" and ended in March, 1948.

Pisces: (The Fishes): The twelfth sign of the zodiac. Its symbol (♓) represents a pair of great sea-horses or sea-lions, yoked together, who dwell in the innermost regions of the sea; symbolical of life after death; of bondage—the inhibiting of self-expression except through others; and of the struggle of the soul within the body. The Sun is in Pisces annually from February 21 to March 20. Astrologically it is the thirty-degree arc immediately preceding the passing of the Sun over the point of the Spring Equinox occupying a position along the Ecliptic from 330° to 360°. It is the "mutable" quality of the element Water: negative, cold, moist, obeying, fruitful; also effeminate, idle, sickly and unfortunate. Ruler: Jupiter; or by some moderns: Neptune. Exaltation: Venus. Detriment: Mercury. Fall: Mercury. Symbolic interpretation: Bondage, captivity; the inhibition of natural expression.

Pisky: See: *Pixie.*

Pistology: A term derived from the Greek *pistis*, faith; hence in general the science of faith or religious belief. A branch of theology specially concerned with faith and its restricted scope, as distinguished from reason.

Pitris: In occult philosophy, the progenitors of the human race. They are instrumental and helpful in the evolution of man, build his body for his incarnation and give him his mind and vital energy. Theosophists know seven classes of pitris (three incorporeal and four corporeal). In general, the "parents" of present-day human individualities (q.v.) are called *solar pitris*, while those of present-day human personalities (q.v.) are referred to as *lunar pitris.*

Pixie, pixy: A fairy-like nature-spirit.

PK: *Psychokinesis* (q.v.).

Planchette: An instrument used by mediums for communicating with the spirits of the dead; a triangular board on rollers, with a pencil under it. The board moves under the hand of the medium, and the pencil writes messages on a paper attached to the underside of the board.

Plane: In occultistic terminology, the range or realm of a given state of consciousness or a state of matter (cf. *plane of existence*).

Planes of existence: All schools of occultism teach that the conscious personality of man lives on after the death of the physical body, and that life in the physical world, in the physical body is merely a plane of existence, after which there follows life on the *astral plane* and then on the *mental plane.*

Planetary ages of man: The ancients called the planets chronocrators, or markers of time. It was assumed that different periods of life are ruled by different planets, as:

Planet	Period	Ages	
Moon—growth	4 years	1-4	the mewling babe
Mercury—education	10 years	5-14	the scholar
Venus—emotion	8 years	15-22	the lover
Sun—virility	19 years	23-42	the citizen
Mars—ambition	15 years	43-57	the soldier
Jupiter—reflection	12 years	58-69	the judge
Saturn—resignation	30 years	70-99	slippers

These appear to correspond to the Seven Ages of Man, as listed by Shakespeare in "As You Like It," which he apparently took from the Chaldeans.

Sepharial suggests a slightly altered set of measures, to include the planets of recent discovery:

Planet	Duration of Years	Age Period
Moon	7	0-7
Mercury	8	7-15
Venus	9	15-24
Sun	10	24-34
Mars	11	35-45
Jupiter	12	46-57
Saturn	13	57-70
Uranus	14	70-84
Neptune	15	84-99
Pluto	16	99-115

Planetary gods: See: *Planetary spirits.*

Plastic essence of matter: In occultism, the world substance (q.v.).

Plastic soul: The Protean soul (q.v.).

Planetary spirits: In theosophical terminology, the seven rulers of the planets ("planetary gods"); they are regarded as emanations and agents of the Absolute.

Pleroma: Literally, Greek for *filling up;* this term was used by the Gnostics to denote the world of light, or the spiritual world of aeons full of divine life.

Plotinism: See: *Neo-Platonism.*

Pluto: Roman god of the infernal regions, identified with the Greek Hades.

Pneuma: Greek for *breath.* Spirit, vital force, or creative fire in its penetration into matter. Sometimes understood as psychic energy, or distinguished as the formative fire-mind and the divinely inspired rational part of man from the more emotional, physical aspect of soul. In early Christian, particularly Gnostic philosophy, *pneuma,* as spirit, is differentiated from *psyche,* or soul.

Pneumatology: In the most general sense, the philosophical or speculative treatment of spirits or souls, including human, divine and those intermediate between God and man.

P'o: In Chinese occult terminology, the passive, negative or earthly part of the human soul, as contrasted with the active, positive or heavenly part called *hun.*

Polarian: The first *root race* (q.v.) in esoteric philosophy. Also called *Adamic.*

Polarity: According to the Rosicrucian Manual, "the predominance of one or the other phase of electrical or magnetic force possessed by any manifestation of creation, and which gives it its distinguished character of positive or negative. . . . This applies to all forms and kinds of creation, for each has its individual and characteristic polarity by which it is distinguished from the other manifestations of its own class and of other classes."

Polong: Malay for *familiar spirit.*

Poltergeist: A noisy, malicious discarnate spirit which causes inexplicable disturbances and moves material objects, especially in certain places and in the presence of a certain person.

Polytheism: Belief in many gods.

Popul Vuh: Literally "Book of Writing on Leaves." The mythology and occult lore of the Quiche Indians of Guatemala.

Poseidon: In Greek mythology, brother of Zeus and god of the sea.

Possession: In occult terminology, the state in which a living person's personality is usurped and his body is controlled by an invading malignant discarnate entity.

Postcognition: The art or faculty of descrying the past.

Posthypnotic suggestion: An order given by the hypnotist to the hypnotized subject, which the latter carries out after awakening without recalling that he was ordered to do so.

Powder of projection: A substance sought by the alchemists for the transmutation of metals into gold.

Powder of sympathy: A magical medicament which is believed to possess the faculty to heal and cure wounds by sympathetic magic—by being applied not to the wound but to the weapon or object which produced the wound.

Pradakshini: The pilgrimage along both banks of the Ganges River, most sacred of all rivers according to the Hindus.

Pradhana: Sanskrit for *primary matter;* the primordial substance or primeval cosmic substance.

Pragmatics: A department of semiotics (q.v.), consisting of the theory and study of the relations between signs and those who produce or receive and understand them. This theory comprehends psychology, sociology, and history of the use of signs, especially of languages.

Prajapati: Sanskrit for *lord of creatures.* A term originally applied to various Vedic gods; it assumed, as early as the Rig Veda, the importance of a first philosophical principle of creation, and later of time as suggestive of gestation and productive periodicity.

Prajna: A Sanskrit term denoting realization, insight into the true and abiding nature of the self, *atman, purusha,* etc.

Prajnana: Sanskrit for *intelligence.*

Prakriti; prakrti: Sanskrit for *Substance* (as opposed to or contrasted with Spirit). The cosmic substance which is the primary source of all things, uncaused cause of phenomenal existence, eternal, all-pervasive, indestructible, emanated from the Absolute.

Pralaya: The dissolution and reabsorption of the universe at the end of a *Kalpa* (q.v.). This is the transcendental phase of consciousness, the passive phase, the potential period when all manifestations are dormant. (See: *Brahma's night.*)

Pramana: A Sanskrit term for "means of acquiring right knowledge."

Prana: Sanskrit for *breath.* In mystic and occult philosophy, the *vital air,* the *Life Principle.*

Pranayama: Sanskrit for *breath-control.* In Yoga practice, a breath exercise considered necessary for proper mental function and development.

Prapatti marga: A Sanskrit term for the way of salvation by a complete and utter surrender to God.

Pranayama: Sanskrit for *holding the breath;* breath control by means of inhalation, suspension, and exhalation. One of the stages in the practice of Yoga.

Prasada: Favor, grace, recognized by some Indian religio-metaphysical systems as divine recompense for *bhakti* (q.v.).

Pratyabhijna: Sanskrit for recognition; particularly the rediscovery or realization that the divine and ultimate reality is within the human soul or self. One phase of the philosophy of the Trika (q.v.).

Pratyahara: The Sanskrit term for the withdrawal of the senses from external objects; one of the stages in the practice of Yoga.

Pratyaksha: A Sanskrit term denoting perception by the spirit.

Pray: In the folklore of Cambodia (Indo-China), an evil spirit.

Prayer flag: Small pennants made of fabric strung by the hundreds across the entrance gates to larger Tibetan cities. Each flutter of the flags in the wind is believed to cause a prayer to be carried across the skies to Buddha.

Prayer wall: In Tibet, a stone roadside shrine, copiously inscribed, often stretching for a quarter of a mile or even more. Passers-by must go by it on the left, in conformity with the Oriental belief that respect is shown to things by keeping them always on the right side of oneself.

Prayer wheel: See: *Wheel of prayer.*

Precipitation of matter: A theory in occultism which claims that a solid body or object can be resolved into its component atoms, passed in this state of dissolution through another solid object and then re-assembled ("precipitated") to its original state.

This theory has been used to explain apports, materializations (q.v.), etc.

Precognition: Knowledge, not obtained by the five human senses, of a future event which could not be known by reasoning or rational inference.

Predictive astrology: That branch of astrology which deals with the methods by which future influences are ascertained.

Precognition: Awareness of knowledge of events before they happen.

Predestination: The doctrine that all events of man's life, even one's eternal destiny, are determined beforehand by Deity.

Pre-existence: The existence of the soul before its incarnation in its present body.

Prehistory: That part of history of which we have no written records, documents or oral accounts, but which is reconstructed from material remains by archeologists and anthropologists.

Premonition: Warning of a future event.

Prescience: Foreknowledge. It suggests preparedness for the exercise of discretion, rather than the fatalistic terror inspired by a prediction.

Presentation: In the narrow sense: anything directly present to a knowing mind such as sense data, images of memory and imagination, emotional states, etc. In the wider sense: any object known by acquaintance rather than by description; for example, an object of perception or memory.

Presentational continuum: The conception of an individual mind as an originally undifferentiated continuum which becomes progressively differentiated in the course of experience.

Presence, Stage of: See: *Dasa-bhumi.*

Pretas: In Hindu terminology, the ghosts of the dead, which are not yet at rest and haunt cemeteries and other places.

Prevision: Visual foreknowledge of future events.

Prima materia: See: *Prime matter.*

Primary truth: A conception or proposition which is dependent for its truth on no other principle in the same order of thought; it may be considered self-evident from common experience, special intuitive insight, or even by postulation; but it is not demonstrated.

Prime matter: The basic substance or essence of all substances which the alchemists considered to be present everywhere as the basic essence which always remains one, homogeneous and unchanged; they identified it with the World Soul (q.v.) as the source of all elements.

Prime mover: In Aristotle's philosophy that which is the first cause of all change and, being first, is not subject to change by any prior agent.

Primum mobile: In Ptolemaic cosmogony, the outermost, or tenth sphere, which in its daily motion carried all of the fixed stars.

Prince of Darkness: In demonography and occultism, a name for Satan or Beelzebub; the devil.

Prince of the Torah: In Jewish mysticism, "the angel who represents the Torah [the Holy Scriptures] in Heaven. The elements, the forces of nature, and the nations, which according to Jewish tradition, are seventy in number, are represented by their respective princes, who are either angels or demons." (M. Buber.)

Principle: A fundamental cause or universal truth; that which is inherent in anything. That which ultimately accounts for being. According to occult philosophy, fundamental aspects of the Universal Reality, which are the primary source of all being, actuality and knowledge.

Process theory of mind: The conception of mind in terms of process in contrast to substance. A mind, according to the process theory, is a relatively permanent pattern preserved through a continuously changing process.

Profane: Outsider, not a member of a specific group, order or fraternity; worldly.

Profane mysteries: Popular occultism.

Prognosis: An astrological term, originally synonymous with *prediction;* usage has attached to it a more conservative meaning, that of "a probability of outcome."

Progressions: An astrological term for alterations in the birth chart aiming to show the changing influences that result from motions of the celestial bodies after birth.

Projection: In occult terminology, the releasing of the astral body from limitations of time and space. (See: *astral projection.*)

Prophecy: Foretelling the future. According to occult teachings anyone who is able to prophesy accurately must be psychically equipped to read the Akashic, or astral, records (cf. *Akasha*). When there is faulty interpretation it is not the astral light which falters but the adept who is not in tune with the vibratory beam.

Prophetic dream: "A dream is prophetic when the dreamer is able to become not only fully conscious upon superior levels, but when he is able to transmit his experiences thereon to his brain and waking consciousness." (G. A. Gaskell.)

Propitiation: The attempt by act or intent of gaining the favor of a god, demon, spirit, etc., removing one's guilt and the divine displeasure. Such acts have taken on innumerable forms: sacrifice of precious possessions, even of human life, of animals, by pilgrimages, tithing, self-imposed asceticism of one kind or another, fastings, rituals, tortures, contrition, etc.

Proselyte: A convert.

Proserpina: The Roman name of Persephone (q.v.).

Protean soul: In occult terminology, the superior astral form or body which the thought of an adept can force to assume any form.

Protective magic: The use of magic formulae, incantations, rituals, etc., for averting or overcoming evil influences.

Psi: "A general term to identify personal factors or processes in nature which transcend accepted laws. It approximates the popular use of the word 'psychic' and the technical one, 'parapsychical.'" (*The Journal of Parapsychology.*)

Psi phenomena: Happenings resulting from the functioning of *psi* (q.v.).

Psyche: In the Greek philosophy prior to the sixth century B.C., the religious factor in man, the indestructible but not immortal soul. In later Greek philosophy, the religious factor in man, closely identified with *nous* (q.v.).

Psychic (*noun*): A medium.

Psychic, psychical (*adjective*): Mental; relating to, emanating from, dealing with or based on the soul or psyche; non-physical.

Psychic body: In spiritualistic terminology, this term is applied to mean either the soul itself or an intermediary between the soul and the physical body.

Psychic force: In spiritualistic terminology, a force emanating from the body of the medium, observable through its manifestations beyond the periphery of the medium's body, without physical contact, subject to the direction and control of the medium. It is also subject to an ebb and flow, depending on factors such as the psychological atmosphere in the seance room, etc.

Psychic healing: The method, believed in by a great many adherents to occult doctrines, of healing and curing by the influence of the mind or thoughts over material nature and natural conditions.

Psychic mind: A Rosicrucian term for *Ego*.

Psychic phenomena: The material manifestations produced by a *medium* or a *sensitive* (q.v.); *psi phenomena* (q.v.).

Psychic Science: Defined by N. Fodor as "a system of facts to demonstrate the existence of spirits independent of the body, and their ability to communicate with humanity."

Psychic self: A Rosicrucian term for the *Ego*.

Psychical Research: The term used in Great Britain for *parapsychology* (q.v.).

Psychism: Psi phenomena (q.v.).

Psychoanalysis: The system and school of psychotherapy originated by Sigmund Freud. This method consists in the use of such procedures as free association, automatic writing and especially dream-analysis to recover forgotten events, suppressed desires and other subconscious items which exert a disturbing influence on the conscious life of an individual. The cure of the psychic disturbances is effected by bringing the suppressed items into the full consciousness of the individual.

Psychograph: An instrument designed to facilitate and test the mediumistic phenomenon of automatic writing (q.v.); it consists of a rotating disk which carries an index over an alphabet.

Psychography: In spiritualism and psychical research, *direct writing* (q.v.). In theosophy, the term is used for "writing under the dictation or the influence of one's 'soul power'" (*The Theosophical Glossary*).

Psychokinesis: The moving of, or in general the exertion of direct influence on a material with any known physical agency or means.

Psychology: The science and study of the human mind, its structure and functions.

Psychometry: The psychic faculty of certain persons to divine events connected with material objects when in close contact with the latter. The material objects are considered to be acting as catalysts for the psi faculty. Occultists call it "reading or seeing" with the inner sight.

Psychopathology: The scientific study of mental disorders.

Psychoplasm: A synonym for *ectoplasm* (q.v.).

Psychosomatic: Relating to, effecting or originating in both mind and body.

Psychotherapy: The science and method of cure of mental and psychosomatic disorders by the use of suggestion, persuasion, rationalization, psychoanalysis, etc. Faith healing (q.v.), too, may be included under this heading.

Psylli: Individuals believed to possess the magic power to charm snakes. (Africa.)

Ptah: A god of ancient Egypt, principle of Light and Life, the pure intellect "which is the ultimate origin of all creation."

P'u: Chinese for *unwrought simplicity;* the Taoist symbol of man's natural state, when his inborn powers have not been tampered with by knowledge or circumscribed by morality.

Pu tung hsin: A Chinese term for the state of unperturbed mind, as a result of "maintaining firm one's will and doing no violence to the vital force" which pervades the body. (Mencius.)

Puja: The Hindu term for worship, religious service.

Pundit: See: *Pandit.*

Purana: One of eighteen or more sacred treatises of India, legendary and allegorical in character, discussing five principal topics, viz., the creation of the universe, its destruction and renovation, the genealogy of gods and patriarchs, the reigns of the Manus, and the history of the solar and lunar races; interspersed are ethical, philosophical, and scientific observations; they are supposed to have been compiled by the poet Vyasa.

Purgation: Spiritual purification, to permit progress toward union with the Deity.

Purification: Any process of ceremonial cleansing after a fault of commission or omission; any of the various disciplines or rituals designed for moral or spiritual cleansing.

Purity, Stage of: See: *Dasa-bhumi.*

Purna: Sanskrit for *filled, satisfied,* used occasionally as a synonym for the Absolute, *brahman.*

Purnatva: Sanskrit for *fullness,* used as descriptive of reality.

Purusha: Sanskrit for *Spirit,* as opposed to or compared with Substance. The Cosmic Spirit; the ultimate principle that regulates, guides, and directs the process of cosmic evolution, the efficient cause of the universe that gives the appearance of consciousness to all manifestations of matter; it is pure spirit, eternal, indestructible, and all-pervasive; it is without activity and attribute, without parts and form; it is the unevolved which does not evolve, the uncaused which is not the cause of any new mode of being.

Purva-Mimamsa: See: *Mimamsa.*

Pyromancy: Divination by means of fire.

Pythoness: In ancient Greece, the oracle of the temple of Delphi. By extension, any seeress.

Quadrant: In astrological terminology, one of the four quarters of the Celestial Figure, representative of the four quarters of the heavens, measured from the cusps of the four angular Houses. The oriental quadrants consist of Houses X to XII inclusive, and IV to VI inclusive. The occidental quadrants, of Houses I to III inclusive, and VII to IX inclusive.

Quadrupedal signs: In astrological terminology, the Signs Aries, Taurus, Leo, Sagittarius and Capricorn, all of which represent quadrupeds. (Those born when these signs ascend were said by the ancient astrologers to have the qualities of such animals: as bold as the lion, or as lustful as the goat, etc.)

Quakerism: The name given to that Christian group officially known as the Society of Friends founded by George Fox (1624-1691). Central principles include: guidance by an inner light (q.v.); freedom from institutional or outward sanctions; the sanctity of silence (q.v.); the simplicity of living; and, commitment to peaceful social relations. Three American groups are: orthodox, Hicksites (liberal) and Wilburites (formalists).

Quaternary: See: *Lower quaternary*.

Querent: The person who asks a question of an oracle, an astrologer, a seer, etc.

Quesited: A term applied in horary astrology to the person or thing that is the subject of an inquiry.

Quetzalcoatl: The feathered-serpent god of the Aztecs; creator of men, god of the wind and of the waning moon.

Quiddity: Essence; that property, quality, etc., which is described in a definition.

Quinanes: An ancient race of giants in Central American folk-lore.

Quintessence: Latin for *fifth essence;* the purest, most highly concentrated form of a nature or essence; originally, in Aristotelianism, the fifth element, found in celestial bodies, distinguished from the four earthly elements.

R

Ra: The sun god of the priests of Heliopolis (Egypt). Later, Ra was combined with Amon, god of Thebes, in Amon-Ra. (Also called *Re.*)

Radical: In astrology, in general, this expression means: pertaining to the radix, or horoscope of birth. In horary astrology, it is employed to indicate a figure which can appropriately be judged in a given matter; one that is likely to give the correct answer.

Radical position: In astrology, a planet's position in a birth horoscope, as distinguished from the transitory or progressed position it occupies at a later date.

Radiesthesia: The term, literally meaning *perception of radiations* or *radiation-sensitivity*, is used by many occultists to explain mysterious phenomena, such as dowsing, psychic healing, etc., by postulating a sensitivity to subtle forces or emanations. (Cf. *od.*)

Radix: In astrology this term is used in two senses: (1) The radical map: the horoscope of birth, the root from which everything is judged. (2) The radical or birth positions of the planets, as distinguished from their progressed or directed positions.

Ragnarok: In Norse and Teutonic cosmogony, the end of the present state of the world, when a new age of righteousness on a new earth will be accomplished by a battle between the gods and the evil giants, in which evil will be overthrown.

Rahu: In Hindu mythology Rahu is a *daitya* (demon) who possessed an appendage like a dragon's tail, and made himself immortal by stealing from the gods some *amrita*—elixir of divine life—which they obtained by churning an ocean of milk. Unable to deprive him of his immortality, Vishnu exiled him from Earth and made of him the constellation Draco: his head is called Rahu, and his tail Ketu. Using his appendage as a weapon, he has ever since waged a destructive war on the denouncers of his robbery, the Sun and the Moon, which he swallows during the eclipse. The fable is presumed to have a mystic or occult meaning.

Rajas: In the Sankhya system of Hindu philosophy, and in theosophical terminology, one of the three constituents of the Cosmic Substance (*prakriti*, q.v.), viz. the activating aspect of Nature without which the other constituents could not manifest their inherent qualities; in Yoga the quality of egoism or selfishness.

Rajayoga: Yoga in its aspect of a philosophy.

Rakahasa: A Sanskrit term for *demon* "that flourishes in the dark."

Ram: See: *Aries*.

Rama: One of the chief Avatars of Vishnu; next to Krishna, the most popular deity of Vishnuism.

Ramayana: A great epic poem of India, ascribed to Valmiki, describing the doings of Rama and his wife Sita, in about 24,000 verses divided into seven books; the first and the last are believed to be comparatively modern additions, but the date of the original books is probably the third or fourth century B.C.; Rama's character is described as that of a perfect man, who bears suffering and self-denial with superhuman patience.

Rapport: A mystic connection between two individuals; although the rapport is usually sympathetic, it may be antipathic, too. In hypnosis, the relationship between the hypnotist and his subject, in which the subject hears the orders of the hypnotist only and is oblivious to all other events around him.

Rashnu: The Zoroastrian spirit of truth, who with Mithra and Sraosha forms a triad and judges the dead.

Rationalization: The mental fabric of explanations, on the ground of known facts and laws, for events, experiences, etc., which would otherwise be inexplicable. (For instance, the explanation of occult experiences in terms of physical laws.) In psychology, the term is used to describe the mind's fabrication of rational argument to justify conduct of which one is really ashamed.

Ray: In ancient Akkadian literature, the source or symbol of the divine power of the gods; the loss of the rays to another god meant loss of supernatural powers and functions.

Re: See: *Ra.*

Rectification: In astrology, the process of verification or correction of the birth moment or ascendant degree of the map, by reference to known events or characteristics pertaining to the native.

Rectified rite: See: *Martinists.*

Recurrence cycle: The period of time required for the recurrence of an event or phenomenon. In astrology, specifically, the periods of time in which a conjunction of any two given planets will recur in approximately the same degree of the zodiac.

Red Dragon: An allegorical symbol in medieval alchemy for man after he has been purified and transmuted spiritually.

Red lion: The alchemical compound or mixture which is believed to have the power to transmute metals into gold.

Red Sect of Lamaism: See: *Ningma.*

Red voodoo sect: That sect of the voodoo cult which practices human sacrifice.

Redintegration: The integral reproduction of a total state of consciousness when an element of it is reproduced.

Referend: The vehicle or instrument of an act of reference. Thus a percept functions as a referend in relation to the perceptual object (the *referent*).

Referent: The object towards which an act of reference is directed. (See: *referend.*)

Refranation: A term used in horary astrology when one of two planets applying to an aspect turns retrograde before the aspect is complete. It is taken as an indication that the matter under negotiation will not be brought to a successful conclusion.

Reincarnation: Rebirth of the personality, the divine essence which is the soul, in a new body, which is on the same level of the physical evolutionary scale. (Rebirth in a body belonging to a different species is called the doctrine of the *transmigration of the soul*—q.v.). The personality in the new body usually has no conscious memory of its previous incarnation. The return to corporeal life after the death of the physical body is regarded by occultists as but a phase in the whole of a single, indivisible life. (Cf. *Samsara.*)

Relic: Object venerated because of its association with a venerated person.

Religious factor: The destiny-determining property of objects, forces, powers, etc., which comprise the world of human experience; any power in the world construed as affecting the span and course of life, destiny or fortune of man and other entities or objects of nature.

Rephaim: A Hebrew term for giants supposed to have lived in primeval times.

Res cogitans: Latin for *thinking thing.* Descartes' designation for thinking substance which along with extended substance (*res extensa*) constitute his dualism. The term presumably designates not only the individual mind which thinks but also the substance which pervades all individual minds.

Retreat: A period of withdrawal for special devotions or meditation, usually in a group under guidance of a teacher or adept; also the place reserved for such activity.

Retrocognition: Knowledge of the past by means or agencies other than the five normal human senses.

Retrograde: The term applied in astrology to an apparent backward motion in the Zodiac of certain planets when decreasing in longitude as viewed from the Earth, due to the rate of change in angular relationship.

Revelation: The communication to man of the Divine Will. This communication has taken, in the history of religions, almost every conceivable form, e.g., the results of lot casting, oracular declarations, dreams, visions, ecstatic experiences (induced by whatever means, such as intoxicants), books, prophets, unusual characters, revered traditional practices, storms, pestilence, etc. The general conception of revelation has been that the divine communication comes in ways unusual, by means not open to the ordinary channels of investigation.

Rhabdic force: The force said to be acting on a *divining rod* (q.v.).

Rhabdomancy: The science, art and practice of handling the divining rod.

Rhapsodomancy: A form of divination, based on a line in a sacred book or book of poetry which strikes the eye when the book is opened, or which is the last line to be pierced by a needle stuck through the closed book.

Rig Veda: The oldest part of the *Vedas* (q.v.), consisting of hymns to the gods.

Ring: In theosophical terminology, a synonym of *cycle*.

Ring of invisibility: A legendary magic ring which is said to make the wearer invisible to ordinary human vision.

Rishi: Sanskrit for *seer;* a sage.

Rising sign: In astrology, the Sign or the subdivision of the Sign which was rising on the eastern horizon at the moment of birth; it is deemed to exercise a strong influence upon the personality and physical appearance of the native.

Rite: A formal or conventional act or series of acts, especially those of a religious or magical character.

Rites of passage: Ceremonies clustering about the great turning points of earthly life or the periods of transition from one status to another (birth, puberty, marriage, death, etc.).

Ritual: A prescribed series or set of ceremonies, rites, acts, words, gestures, etc., determined by considerations of tradition and symbolism.

Root race: "Life as cultural complex is charted by the great continents or root races through which the human life stream establishes itself on the globe. . . . The great ages of mankind are the progressive epochs of dominant and cultural complexes. They are centered geographically in the continental areas where the streaming divine sparks converge into a particular aspect of experience and thereupon constitute a root race. There are seven of such primary aggregations according to the esoteric tradition . . . namely the Polarian [or Adamic], the Hyperborean, the Lemurian, the Atlantean, the Aryan, and two still to come." (Marc Edmund Jones.)

Rosicrucian Order (Ancient Mystical Order Rosae Crucis—A.M.O.R.C.): Defined by the Rosicrucian Order itself as "a worldwide fraternal organization, established and operating on a lodge system. It expounds a system of metaphysical and physical philosophy intended to awaken the dormant, latent faculties of the individual whereby he may utilize to a better advantage his natural talents and lead a happier and more useful life. It accomplishes this by a method of personal instruction and guidance." The word *Rosicrucian* is derived from the Latin *Rosae Crucis*, meaning *of the Rosy Cross;* the traditional symbol of the order is a cross with a single red rose in the center. The Order has its traditional origin in the Great White Brotherhood of Egypt (15th century B.C.).

Round: In theosophical terminology, the passage of the immortal part of man (*monad*) through the complete chain of planes of existence.

Ruach: In Kabbalistic terminology, the divine soul in man.

Rudra: A storm god of Vedic Hinduism, representing the destructive effects of the storm.

Ruh: The Arabic equivalent of the Hebrew *ruach,* the divine soul of man—the Mind.

Ruh i Basit: The Sufi term for the Universal Soul, the efficient aspect of God, which animates the whole universe and is present in every soul.

Ruler: An astrological term, at times loosely-applied, principally concerned with a schematic arrangement of the Signs, whereby certain planets are deemed to have special potency or congeniality in a certain sign or signs. The entire subject of rulership is involved in much controversy, particularly since the modern discovery of additional planets for which there is no place in the ancient scheme of rulerships. It is recommended, in general, to speak of the *Lord* of a *House* and the *Ruler* of a *Sign.* The Lord of a House is deemed to be the Ruler of the Sign that occupies the cusp. The Lord of the Nativity, or as often termed the Ruler of the Horoscope, is variously the most strongly placed planet in the map, especially that planet which is in the First House and close to the ascending degree. Lacking a planet so placed, the Ruler of the ascending sign is the Lord of the Nativity.

Rulership, geographical: For the interpreting of horary figures, astrologers consider certain countries and cities to be under the rulership of different signs.

Ruminant signs: A term applied in astrology to the signs Aries, Taurus, Capricorn.

Runes: Early Germanic letters, believed to possess magical powers.

Rupa: Sanskrit for *form*. (Cf. *nama-rupa*.)

Sabbath: See: *Witches' Sabbath.*

Sabbatic goat: Baphomet (q.v.).

Sacerdotalism: In general, any religious system revolving about a priestly order. The term, when employed in a derogatory sense, means the unwholesome preference for ecclesiastical and sacramental observances in contrast to the more valid personal and moral values.

Sacramental meal: A feature found in many ancient religions; in some instances, the purpose of the meal was to establish a "table fellowship" with the deity, in others an actual absorption of the god by the worshipper in partaking of the sacred food in which the deity was believed to be present. (Cf. *theophagy.*)

Sacred science: In occult terminology, the esoteric philosophical secrets taught and disclosed as a part of the initiation to the highest degree in the mysteries (q.v.).

Sacrifice: A ceremonial offering to a god, demon or other superhuman or supernatural being.

Saddle-back present: That part of time called *present*, conceived as having small duration.

Sadhaka: A Sanskrit term meaning a spiritual seeker of truth and enlightenment.

Sadhana: A Sanskrit term for spiritual effort or quest of enlightenment. In Tantric Buddhism, a ceremony by the performance of which the worshipper can render visible any god he desires and is enabled to obtain control of the deity. In Hinduism, the means through which the Hindu student of esoteric sciences attains to *samadhi* (q.v.).

Sadhu: A Sanskrit term for a man who has dedicated himself to the quest for spiritual enlightenment, renouncing all worldly goods and comfort.

Sagittarius (The Archer): The ninth sign of the zodiac. In Hindu astrology: Dhanus. Its symbol (♐) represents an arrow and a section of a bow, typifying aspiration. It is usually pictured as the Centaur: half horse, half man—representing the conflict between the philosophical mind and the carnal instinct of conquest; also aspiration supported by effort that aims at the stars. Said to have been named for the Babylonian god of war. The Sun is in Sagittarius annually from November 23 to December 21. Astrologically it is the thirty-degree arc immediately preceding the Sun's passing over the Tropic of Capricorn, occupying a position along the Ecliptic from 240° to 270°. It is the "mutable" quality of the element Fire: positive, hot, dry, changeable, bicorporeal, obeying. Ruler: Jupiter. Detriment: Mercury. Symbolic interpretation: The centaur; an arrow with a short section of the bow, the symbol of enthusiasm and effort, aiming at the stars.

Saguna: Sanskrit for "possessed of qualities"; predicated of the Absolute from the exoteric point of view of the worshipper, in the philosophy of Sankara. (Cf. *nirguna*.)

Saguna Brahman: In the teachings of Yoga, the creatively active aspect of the Deity, endowed with specific attributes and powers. In Saguna Brahman there appear the features of Ishwara (q.v.).

Saivism: See: *Shivaism*.

Sakti, Saktism: See: *Shakti, Shaktism*.

Sakya: A semi-reformed sect of Lamaism (Tibetan Buddhism); called the Multiple-Colored Sect.

Sakya Muni; Sakyamuni: Sanskrit for *Great Sage*. A name of Gautama Buddha, founder of Buddhism.

Salamander: An *elemental* (q.v.) of the element Fire.

Salamander's feather: The name given by alchemists to asbestos.

Salik: The Sufi term for a seeker of the mystic union with God.

Sama Veda: That part of the *Vedas* (q.v.) which consists of priests' ritual chants.

Samadhi: Sanskrit for *putting together*. Profound meditation, absorption in the spirit. The final stage in the practice of Yoga, in which the individual becomes one with the object of meditation, thus attaining a condition of superconsciousness and unqualified blissfulness, which is called *moksha*.

Samael: In the Kabbalah, the prince of the spirits of evil.

Sambhu: In Hindu mythology, Siva in the aspect of the Bounteous.

Samkhya: See: *Sankhya.*

Samma Sambuddha: A term used by Buddhist mystics for a person's sudden remembering of all of his past incarnations, through the mastery of Yoga.

Sammael: Hebrew name, used in post-biblical times, of Satan.

Samothracian mysteries: See: *Phrygian mysteries.*

Samru: In Persian occultism, the bird of immortality.

Samsara: In Hinduism and occult terminology, the wheel of life, the chain of birth and rebirth, discarnation and reincarnation —endless except for self-realization (q.v.).

Samskara: Sanskrit for *putting together.* Mental impression, memory. Also the effects of *karma* (q.v.) as shaping one's life.

Sanga: Sanskrit for *attachment,* especially to material things, or entanglement in earthly cares, considered an impediment to spiritual attainment or *moksha* (q.v.).

Sankhya: Perhaps the oldest of the major systems of Indian philosophy, founded by Kapila (sixth century B.C.). Originally not theistic, it is realistic in epistemology, dualistic in metaphysics, assuming two moving ultimates, Cosmic Spirit (*purusha*) and Cosmic Substance (*prakriti*), both eternal and uncaused. *Prakriti* possesses the three qualities or principles of *sattva, rajas, tamas,* first in equipoise. When this is disturbed, the world in its multifariousness evolves in conjunction with *purusha* which becomes the plurality of selves in the process. The union (*samyoga*) of spirit and matter is necessary for world evolution, the inactivity of the former needing the verve of the latter, and the non-intelligence of that needing the guidance of conscious *purusha.* Successively, *prakriti* produces *mahat* or *buddhi, ahamkara, manas,* the ten *indriyas,* five *tanmatras* and five *mahabhutas* (q.v.).

Sannyasin: A Sanskrit term for a holy man, an ascetic, who has dedicated himself completely to the quest for *moksha.*

Sanskrit: The ancient language of India, language of the Vedas and other sacred and classical texts of Hinduism; the linguistic ancestor of the modern *prakritas* or vernaculars.

Saoshyant: A Zoroastrian term used variously in the meaning of priest or apostle, who will aid in establishing the age of peace and righteousness in the world.

Sarasvati: Hindu goddess of learning, wife of Brahma.

Saros: (1) A Chaldean and Babylonian interpretation of a cycle of 60 days as 60 years. (2) 60 sixties, or 3,600. (3) A lunar cycle of 6,585.32 days—223 lunations; or 18 years, 11⅛ days.

Sarvakartrtva: Sanskrit for *all-makingness.* Descriptive of the principle of all-powerfulness as the ultimate principle in the universe, conceived dynamically.

Sat: Sanskrit for *Pure Being.* The active emanation of the transcendental aspect of the Ultimate Principle.

Satanic imp: See: *Imp.*

Satanism: The worship of Satan, principle of evil.

Satchitananda: A Sanskrit term (literally *being-consciousness-bliss*) for the Divine State in which pure bliss is attained by knowledge and being the Self.

Satori: The Japanese Zen Buddhist term for "enlightenment," as the culmination of meditation.

Satsampat: In Hindu philosophy, right conduct, which consists of the six acquirements, viz. tranquillity, self-restraint, tolerance, endurance, faith, and mental equipoise.

Sattva: Sanskrit for *being, existence, reality, true essence;* one of the three constituents of the Cosmic Substance (*prakriti*), viz. the illuminating aspect of Nature that reveals all manifestations; in Yoga, the quality of purity or goodness.

Satya loka: In Hinduism and occult terminology, the world or plane of absolute purity and wisdom, the abode of the gods.

Satya yuga: Sanskrit for *age of truth;* the first age (*yuga*) of the *manvantara.* The *golden age,* which lasted 1,728,000 of our years (the first four-tenths of the entire *manvantara*).

Satyr: One of a class of woodland deities of Greek-Roman mythology, represented by the Greeks as a human figure with a horse's ears and tail, and by the Romans as a human figure with a goat's ears, tail, legs and budding horns.

Savitar: The Vedic sun god; also called Savitri.

Scales: See: *Libra.*

Scapegoat: In Biblical times, one of the two goats upon which the sins of the entire Jewish people during the year just ended were loaded by the high priest in a symbolic ceremony on the Day of Atonement; the two goats were led forth or sent out into the wilderness to die and thus bring expiation for those sins.

Scarab: The image or likeness of the scarabaeus beetle, symbol of resurrection in Egyptian religion.

Scholasticism: The school of Western learning, especially in the fields of philosophy and theology, originating in the ninth century and ending in the fifteenth century; two outstanding features of this school are its intimate association with Catholic theology and its rigorous logical formalism.

Sciomancy: Communication with the shadows of the dead; divination by observing shadows.

Scorpion: See: *Scorpio.*

Scorpio (The Scorpion): The eighth sign of the zodiac. Its symbol (♏) resembles that of Virgo, but with an arrow on the tail—doubtless to represent the sting. It is symbolized by the asp or serpent, harking back to the serpent of the Garden of Eden, and indicating that the will governs or is governed by the reproductive urge. It is sometimes symbolized by the Dragon, and is frequently linked with the constellation Aquilla—the Eagle. The Sun is in Scorpio annually from October 23 to November 22. Astrologically it is the second thirty-degree arc after the Sun's passing of the Fall Equinox, occupying a position along the Ecliptic from 210° to 240°. It is the "fixed" quality of the element Water: negative, nocturnal, cold, moist, watery, mute, phlegmatic. Ruler: Mars. Exaltation: Uranus. Detriment: Venus. Fall: Moon. Symbolic interpretation: The legs and tail of a scorpion; the tail with the sting, the serpent.

Scrier: A crystal-gazer; one who practices *scrying* (q.v.).

Scrying: Divination by crystal-gazing or, in general, by gazing at shining surfaces.

Seance: A session conducted by a spiritualist medium, or attended by at least one person of mediumistic powers, for the purpose of establishing communication with the dead or of witnessing supernormal phenomena.

Second death: In occultism, the dissolution or disintegration of remains of man which dwell in the *kamaloka* (q.v.) after the death of the physical body.

Second sight: The ability for abnormal perception over a distance in time and space, often in the form of symbolical visions; especially the ability to foresee future events.

Secret doctrine: The esoteric teachings which Marc Edmund Jones defines as "arcane wisdom distinguished from secular knowledge because it cannot be told or learned in ordinary fashion, but instead must be acquired by a direct experience of its transcendental insights."

Secret Wisdom: Occult knowledge, esoteric philosophy; the magic art.

Seer: One who sees; a crystal-gazer; a person endowed with second sight; one who foresees future events—a prophet; in astrological terminology, one whose extrasensory perceptions enable him to visualize the ultimate effects that will result from the cosmic causes portrayed in a birth Figure.

Seiktha: In Burmese folklore, a tree spirit, usually malignant.

Seker: In Egyptian occultism, the haw-headed god of the underworld.

Self: See: *Ego.*

Self-attenuation: The *fana* (q.v.) of Sufis.

Self-awareness: The awareness of one's existence as an individual.

Self-consciousness: The knowledge by the self of itself.

Self-effacement: See: *Fana.*

Selfhood: The unique individuality possessed by a self or a person.

Self-realization: The comprehensive, permanent and harmonious realization of one's potentialities.

Self-Realization Fellowship: A non-sectarian organization, founded in 1920 by the late Paramhansa Yogananda. The Fellowship teaches Yoga methods for harmonizing man's physical, mental and spiritual natures. Its headquarters is in Los Angeles, California, and has 100 branches and churches in America, Europe and India. Its president is Rajasi Janakananda.

Semantics: The study of the meaning of words, signs and symbols.

Seminal essence: In the terminology of medieval alchemists, the *quintessence* (q.v.).

Semiotic: A general theory of signs and their applications, especially in language; developed and systematized within Scientific Empericism. Three branches: pragmatics, semantics, syntactics (q.v.).

Sen-rin: In Japanese mystic lore, hermits of the mountains, masters of all magic arts.

Sensation body: The name given by many occultists to the *etheric body*, since they claim that the physical body has sensation only when united with the etheric body.

Sensitive: A person who possesses psychic powers but not necessarily the ability to communicate with the spirits of the dead. Not synonymous with *medium*. (A medium may or may not be a sensitive.)

Sentience: Consciousness at a rudimentary sensory level.

Sepher Yetzirah: See: *Yetzirah*.

Sephiroth: A Hebrew term for "the mystical and organically related hierarchy of the ten creative powers emanating from God, constituting, according to the kabalistic system, the foundation of the existence of the world." (M. Buber: *Tales of the Hasidim*.) The ten *Sephiroth* are: 1. The Divine Crown (*Kether*); 2. The Divine Wisdom (*Hokhmah*); 3. The Intelligence of God (*Binah*); 4. The Divine Love or Mercy (*Hesed*); 5. The Divine Power of judgment and retribution (*Gevurah* or *Din*); 6. The Divine Compassion (*Rahamin*) which mediates between God's Power of judgment and His Mercy; 7. The Lasting Endurance or Firmness of God (*Netsah*); 8. God's Majesty or Splendor (*Hod*); 9. The Foundation of all active forces in God (*Yesod*); 10. The Kingdom of God (*Malkhuth*), which the Zohar usually describes as the mystical archetype of Israel's community. (The above terms are based on the interpretations given by G. G. Scholem in *Major Trends in Jewish Mysticism*. Other authorities occasionally adopt different terminologies. Thus, the fourth of the Sephiroth is frequently called *Tiphereth*, Beauty.)

Seraph: In certain occult disciplines, a *master* (q.v.) who initiates acolytes or neophytes in the greater mysteries.

Seraphim: Winged guardians of God's throne, highest in the hierarchy of angels. (From the Hebrew word *Saraph*—plural: *Saraphim*.)

Serapis: An Egyptian deity of the Ptolemaic period, a combination of Osiris and Apis.

Set: The Egyptian god of the atmosphere, adversary and murderer of Osiris. He was represented as a human figure with the head of an animal of an unknown species.

Seven magical works: In medieval occultism, works of magic were classified in the following seven groups: Works of light and riches, works of mystery and divination, works of science and skill, works of retribution and punishment, works of love, works of intrigue, works of malediction and death.

Shabda: Sanskrit for *sound*. As a philosophical term, it denotes a metaphysical concept: The Cosmic or Divine Word, a verbal testimony, a valid source of knowledge.

Shaivism (Shivaism, Sivaism): One of the three great divisions of modern Hinduism (the other two being Vishnuism and Shaktism); the Shaivas identify Shiva—rather than Brahma and Vishnu —with the Supreme Being, and are exclusively devoted to his worship, regarding him as the creator, preserver, and destroyer of the universe.

Shakti: A Sanskrit word, meaning *power, strength, might*, of feminine gender; in Tantric (see *Tantra*) literature the female generative power of energy in the universe, worshipped by the religious as the wife of some deity or other, e.g., as *Durga*, wife of Shiva. (See *Shaktism*.) In occult terminology, *Shakti* or *Sakti* is the crown of the astral light (q.v.).

Shaktism: The name of one of the three great divisions of modern Hinduism (the other two being Shaivism and Vishnuism); the Shaktas worship Shakti—rather than Shiva and Vishnu—and regard it as the embodiment of the power that supports all that lives and which upholds the universe; Shakti is portrayed as the female aspect of the Ultimate Principle, and deified as the wife of Shiva.

Shaman: Originally, the word means a medicine-man or priest-magician of certain primitive Siberian tribes. The term is generally used now to designate any tribal magician practicing magic rites aimed at influencing superhuman or disembodied entities.

Shamanism: A primitive cult or religion which believes in communication with and influence over discarnate intelligences. The spiritualism of primitive races.

Shamash: In Babylonian mythology, god of the sun and of divination. The Assyrian all-seeing god of right and justice.

Shambalah: The sacred island of esoteric tradition, believed to have been situated in the present Gobi desert in Asia. According to the teachings of several occult schools, including the theosophists, Shambalah is a place or town in the Himalayas.

Shambalah force: In occult terminology, a beneficent cosmic force which enhances good emotions in the morally and spiritually just, but at the same time also stimulates the evil emotions of the bad.

Shang-ti: Chinese for *The Lord of Heaven.*

Sharpness of the eagle: The name of metallic vinegar or essence of mercury in medieval alchemy.

Shekhinah: Hebrew for *indwelling.* The presence of God, of the Divine Mind, among mortals. In Rosicrucian terminology, the name of a triangular altar in the Rosicrucian temple.

Shen: Chinese for *unfathomable spiritual power.* Also, the designation of the Spirits of Heaven, which include Shang-ti (q.v.), the sun, the moon, the stars, wind, rain, etc.

Sheng: Chinese for *sage;* a high adept, a spiritual guide.

Shen jen: Chinese for *the spiritual man,* one who has reached a state of mystical union with the universe, or "who has not separated from the pure and the mysterious." (Chang Tzu, fourth century B.C.)

Sheol: Hebrew for *pit* or *grave.* The nether-world, a dark and dreary underground dwelling place of the dead where their spirits find deep sleep, forgetfulness, silence and destruction.

Shingon: The Japanese sect of Buddhism which claims that its esoteric doctrine was inspired by Vairochana, the greatest of all Buddhas who came to this earth.

Shintia: Japanese for *god-body*, the Shintoist name of material objects in which the divine spirit is said to dwell.

Shinto: The Japanese religion based on the worship of spirits and ancestors.

Ship of the dead: The phantom ship which according to the folklore of many sea-coast races, sails through the air to take away the souls of the dying.

Shi-tenno: In Japanese terminology, the four guardians of the cardinal points of the compass.

Shiva: In Hindu religious doctrines, the Destroyer, one of the three aspects of Ishwara, the triune Personal God (the other two are Brahma, the Creator, and Vishnu, the Preserver), the destroyer of the prison in which man's spirit is held captive. To the devotees of Shiva (see *Shaivism*), the universe is merely a form assumed by Shiva.

Shivaism: See: *Shaivism.*

Shivasvarupa: Sanskrit for *form of Shiva.* The universe as merely a form assumed by Shiva (q.v.).

Shofar: The horn (ram's horn) which is sounded in the Jewish houses of worship, especially on the Hebrew New Year. According to Jewish mystic tradition, a blast on the *shofar* will herald in the coming of the Messiah.

Shraddha: An ancestral rite performed all over India at the death of a person and from time to time thereafter, to provide the ancestral spirit with a new body and to aid it in its progress from lower worlds to higher ones and back to earth.

Shu shu: The ancient Chinese system of magic, divination and occult practices, including astrology, dream interpretation, the art of coordinating human affairs by the active and passive principles of the universe (*yin yang*) and the Five Elements (*wu hsing*), fortune telling by the use of the stalks of the divination plant and the tortoise shell, and miscellaneous methods such as dream interpretation, the regulation of forms and shapes of buildings, etc.

Sibylline Books: Ancient, mythical and inspired utterances of prophecy consulted in times of calamity. Their destruction led to composite and forged versions.

Sibylline Oracles: A group of Jewish and Christian writings dating from the second century B.C. to the third century A.D., written in Homeric style, and in imitation of the lost Sibylline Books. They included prophecies of future events, of the fate of eminent persons, of cities and kingdoms.

Siddha: In Hindu mystic and occultistic terminology, a man who possesses supernatural powers.

Siddhi: Sanskrit for *supernatural power*. Specifically, the super-human physical powers attained through Yoga.

Sidereal: Relating to or originating from the stars.

Sideromancy: Divination by observing straws placed on a piece of red-hot iron.

Sign: In astrology, one of the twelve divisions of the Zodiac. The annual revolution of the Earth round the Sun is divided into the 360° of a circle; the subdivisions of the circle into 12 equal arcs, distinguished by names, are known as the Signs of the Zodiac. They no longer bear any relationship to the constellations of the same name. (Cf. *house.*) The 12 Signs are: Aries, Taurus, Gemini, Cancer, Leo, Virgo, Libra, Scorpio, Sagittarius, Capricorn, Aquarius, Pisces. These twelve signs are generally divided into four basic groups: The Inspirational Group—the *Fire* signs; the Emotional Group—the *Water* signs; the Mental Group—the *Air* signs; the Practical Group—the *Earth* signs. These are termed the Elements, or Triplicities—since three signs are embraced in each group, as follows:

	Cardinal	*Fixed*	*Mutable*
Fire:	Aries	Leo	Sagittarius
Water:	Cancer	Scorpio	Pisces
Air:	Libra	Aquarius	Gemini
Earth:	Capricorn	Taurus	Virgo

Another classification into four groups representing the four seasons, is known as the *Trinities*:

Intellectual (Spring)	*Maternal* (Summer)	*Reproductive* (Autumn)	*Serving* (Winter)
1. Aries	4. Cancer	7. Libra	10. Capricorn
2. Taurus	5. Leo	8. Scorpio	11. Aquarius
3. Gemini	6. Virgo	9. Sagittarius	12. Pisces

Key words often associated with the twelve Signs are:

Aries:	Aspiration	Libra:	Equilibrium
Taurus:	Integration	Scorpio:	Creativity
Gemini:	Vivification	Sagittarius:	Administration
Cancer:	Expansion	Capricorn:	Discrimination
Leo:	Assurance:	Aquarius:	Loyalty
Virgo:	Assimilation:	Pisces:	Appreciation

Silence: The basis of worship according to the teachings of the Society of Friends (Quakers); as God speaks to each in the spirit of each worshipper, each must be prepared to hear Him, and His message will come to those who are silent, ready to receive it.

Silent Watchers: In the esoteric philosophy of theosophy, this term is used to refer to the spiritual guides of the worlds.

Silver Age: The *Tretya Yuga* (q.v.).

Simulacrum (plural: *simulacra*): A likeness or copy of an original; applied especially to a perceptual image which copies its object. (Cf. *effluvium theory*.)

Simultaneity: Co-existence in time. The condition of belonging to the same time. As two or more events observed as simultaneous may actually take place at different moments, it is useful to distinguish between subjective and objective simultaneity. (Cf. *future*.)

Sirr: In Sufi terminology, conscience, regarded as a pure possibility of consciousness, void of contents.

Siva: See: *Shiva*.

Sixth sense: A vague and variously defined term for that faculty, considered by occultists to be latent in all human beings, which enables certain individuals to have or acquire awareness or knowledge which cannot be explained in terms of the five normal human senses. The *psi faculty* studied by parapsychology.

Skin writing: Writing appearing on the skin of a medium and remaining visible there for periods of time varying from a few minutes to a few hours. Also called *dermography*.

Slate-writing: A form of direct writing (q.v.) where the messages from the spirit world are recorded on a slate held in the hands of both the medium and the querent.

Society of Friends: The official name of the movement more commonly known as *Quakerism* (q.v.).

Sod: A Hebrew word for a religious mystery.

Solar mysteries: Self-acquired esoteric knowledge, verified by him who acquires it.

Solar pitris: The progenitors of human individualities.

Solipsism: The metaphysical doctrine that the individual self of the solipsistic philosopher is the whole of reality and that the external world and other persons are representations of that self and have no independent existence.

Sol-om-on: The name of the Sun in three languages; a mystic expression of light, knowledge, understanding.

Solomon's mirror: A steel plate polished to high brilliance, treated according to certain prescribed magic rituals, used for divinatory ceremonial magic.

Solomon's Seal: Two interlaced triangles, the angles of which form the six-pointed star. Often one of the triangles is dark and the other light, symbolizing the union of soul and body. According to occult symbology the apex of the emblem represents the human head or intelligence; the two upper outstretched points, sympathy with everything that lives; the two lower, human responsibility; the angle at the bottom, pointing earthward, procreative power—the cryptograph, in its entirety, denoting complete individuality or human entity. (Also called *Solomon's sign.*)

Solomon's sign: See: *Solomon's Seal.*

Solomon's Temple: In occult literature the human body, as developed by divine principle, is referred to as Solomon's Temple. (The expression refers to the great temple built in Jerusalem by Solomon, son of David, by Bathsheba, King of Israel in the tenth century B.C., which has been given many symbolic interpretations.)

Soma: A plant, the juice of which was the favorite drink of the Vedic gods and was used in Hindu temples to induce trance and give supernatural powers. *Soma* is also the name of a Vedic god.

Somatic: Pertaining to the physical body or bodily organism.

Somnambulism: Sleep-walking; the performing of certain actions in sleep, without recollection of such actions upon awakening.

Son of light: A practitioner of *white magic* (q.v.).

Soniferous ether: The *Akasha* (q.v.).

Soothsayer: A diviner; a person able to foretell future events.

Soothsaying: Divination of future events.

Sophia: The Holy Wisdom of the Gnostic doctrines.

Sorcerer: A practitioner of black magic for evil purposes or selfish ends, who sold his soul to Satan or another form of the Prince of Darkness in exchange for his services and assistance for a determined period of time.

Sorceress: A female sorcerer.

Sorcery: Black magic; the use of supernatural powers for evil or selfish ends.

Sortilege: Divination by drawing or casting lots.

Soul: The divine, immortal part of man. The *psyche* of the Greek philosophers, the *nephesh* of the Hebrew Bible. According to occult philosophy, the vital principle ("breath of life") which all living beings possess.

Soul of the world: See: *World Soul.*

Soul-stuff: Impersonal supernatural power in general, or the subtle, diffuse spiritual essence associated with a particular human being or object. (Cf. *astral body, aura.*)

Sovereign Grand Architect of the Universe, The: The name used in Freemasonic terminology to refer to the Deity; written as T∴S∴G∴A∴O∴T∴U∴.

Spagyric art: A term often used in literature for *alchemy.*

Space-Time: The four-dimensional continuum including the three dimensions of space (length, width and height) and one of time; the unity of space and time.

Spark: According to Jewish mystic tradition, before the creation of our world, the divine light-substance burst into sparks which fell into the lower depths and filled the "shells" of the creatures of the world; the vital essence.

Specious present: The psychological or felt present, a spread of duration embraced within the mind's momentary experience. Contrasts with the physical present which is an ideal limit or boundary between the past and the future.

Spectre: A ghost or ghostly apparition.

Speculative Freemasonry: Modern Freemasonry, in which the members carry on the arts of building craft in a symbolic form.

Speculum: Latin for *mirror.* Any shiny object used for crystal-gazing and other forms of scrying (q.v.).

Spell: Spoken or written words, incantations, or magical symbols, believed to have magical, supernatural powers and effects.

Spermatic word: A Stoic term for Primary Being, the creative force of the universe, which contains the seed or germ of all things.

Spheres: Divisions of the non-material world, in the spatial as well as in the spiritual sense. (See also *music of the spheres.*)

Sphinx: In Greek and Egyptian mythology, a monster with a human head and a body composed of parts of various animals. The most famous sphinx in Greek mythology was that of Thebes in Boetia, mentioned by Hesiod. It was symbolic of the fixed types of the four elements and also had an astrological significance: the body of a bull—Taurus; the feet and tail of a lion—Leo; the wings of the eagle—Scorpio; a human head—Aquarius. Variations are found in all parts of the ancient world, showing its art influence upon those who knew naught of its symbolic significance.

Spirit: The Divine Particle, the vital essence, the innermost principle, the true actuating and activating element in life. Also, any disembodied or incorporeal conscious being in man's invisible environment active for good or ill in human affairs.

Spirit body: See: *Astral body.*

Spirit helper: A spirit guide, guardian spirit or familiar spirit (q.v.).

Spirit lights: Luminous phenomena, ascribed by spiritualists to discarnate intelligences.

Spirit photograph: A photograph, made at a seance, showing what spiritualists believe to be the astral form of a dead person.

Spirit-rapping: The rapping noises, usually heard at spiritualistic seances, through which the spirits of the departed are believed to communicate with the living. (Cf. *table-turning.*)

Spiritism: The French form of *spiritualism* (q.v.), based on the belief in continued life of the conscious personality after death and in the possibility of communicating with the spirits of the deceased, but including among its principles also the belief in reincarnation, which is rejected by spiritualism. Spiritism is founded on the teachings of Hypolyte Leon Denizard Rivail of France (1804-1869), known to his followers under the name of Allan Kardec. (In France and other European countries, the word *spiritisme, Spiritismus,* etc. is used to denote both spiritism and spiritualism.)

Spirits of the elements: The *elementals* (q.v.).

Spiritual man: The term may be applied by many occult philosophies to designate a human being who has attained to the divine principle of wisdom and is therefore immune to the ills of the flesh.

Spiritual self: In occult philosophy, an English term for the Sanskrit *purusha* (q.v.).

Spiritualism: Defined by the National Spiritualist Association of America as "the Science, Philosophy and religion of continuous life, based upon the demonstrated fact of communication, by means of mediumship, with those who live in the Spirit World." Spiritualism rejects the belief in physical reincarnation, but teaches that death is a new birth into a spiritual body, without any change in individuality and character, and without impairment of memory.

Spiritualist: A believer in *spiritualism* (q.v.).

Spiritus rector: Latin for *ruling spirit*. In the terminology of medieval alchemists, the *philosopher's stone* (q.v.) or the *elixir of life* (q.v.).

Spodomancy: Divination by examining the ashes of a sacrifice for omens.

Spook: A ghostly apparition.

Sprite: A nature-spirit; a ghost or spook.

Spunkie: A malignant goblin which delights in attracting travellers who have lost their way, by letting them see a light, and lures them into a morass or over a precipice.

Sraosha: A Zoroastrian deity, forming a triad with Mithra and Rashnu. He protects the faithful and fights the demons.

Srei ap: In the folklore of Cambodia (Indo-China), a demon feeding on human flesh.

Stages, Ten: See: *Dasa-bhumi*.

Stewards of Heaven: The seven Olympic Spirits (q.v.).

Sthula sharira: Sanskrit for *physical body* (q.v.)., conceived as consisting of five elements; the gross body which perishes after physical death.

Stichomancy: Divination by means of a passage picked from a book at random.

Stigmata: The appearance, inexplicable by ordinary human science, of wounds or markings, especially the wounds of the Crucifixion, on the bodies of mystics and sensitives.

Stolas: In demonography, a general of the infernal empire, a demon who teaches mankind astronomy and the properties of precious stones.

Stolisomancy: Divination from the manner of dressing; the belief that the way in which certain articles of clothing are put on or worn determines or produces certain events affecting the wearer.

Stomach of the ostrich: The name of vitriol in medieval alchemy.

Subconscious mind: According to the theory of psychoanalysis, a compartment of the mind which exists below the threshold of consciousness. The subconscious, though not directly accessible to introspection (q.v.), is capable of being tapped by special techniques such as random association, dream-analysis, automatic writing, etc.

Sublimation: In psychoanalytic terminology, the psychological mechanism which consists in the discovery of a substitute object for the expression of a basic instinct or feeling.

Subliminal: Unconscious, below the threshold of consciousness.

Subliminal self: The term used by psychical researchers to designate the subconscious personality.

Substance: That which is present in an entity as the cause of its being. In occult philosophy, a distinction is made between material and spiritual substances. (Theosophy speaks also of a psychic substance.)

Subtle body: In the terminology of *Yoga*, that essential part of the human individuality which survives physical death and continues to be reborn in the *wheel of life* (q.v.). It is considered to be composed of seventeen elements: five senses of perception, five senses of action, five vital energies, mind (*manas*) and intellect (*buddhi*). It is in general identical with the term *etheric double* (q.v.) of other schools of occultism.

Subtler planes: The planes of existence after and above the physical worldly existence (astral plane, mental plane, etc.).

Succuba: The same as *succubus*.

Succubus: A term applied to designate a demon, the astral body of a dead person or of a witch, which takes the form of a woman and has sexual intercourse with mortal men.

Sufism: A system of Mohammedan mysticism, arising chiefly in Persia. It offers steps toward union with God, as repentance, abstinence, renunciation, poverty, patience, trust. Love is the keynote to the Sufi ethics.

Summerland: The Spiritualist term for the dwelling places of the disembodied spirits.

Sunya; sunyata: Sanskrit for *void, nothingness*. In occult terminology, the objective universe seen as an illusion. (See: *sunya-vada*).

Sunya-vada: Sanskrit for *void-theory*. A Buddhist theory (*vada*) holding the world to be void (*sunya*) or unreal. According to it, the phenomenal world has no reality; yet the world underlying it defies description, also because of our inability to grasp the thing-in-itself (*svabhava*). All we know is its dependence on some other condition, its so-called "dependent origination." Thus, nothing definite being able to be said about the real, it is, like the apparent, as nothing, in other words, *sunya*, void.

Superior planets: In astrology, the planets outside of the Earth's orbit (Mars, Jupiter, Saturn, Uranus, Neptune and Pluto).

Superior world: In Kabbalistic and occult terminology, the world of Idea or Mind.

Superman: A higher type of humanity, the goal of human evolution. (The word is the translation of the German *Übermensch*, introduced by Nietzsche.)

Supernatural: Not explicable by or contrary to known and established laws of Nature.

Superstition: This word originally meant survivals of extinct, defeated religions. Today it is generally applied by opponents of occultism to all occult beliefs and in general to beliefs in the existence of superhuman or supernatural forces and beings. It is frequently applied also to religious beliefs of ancient peoples and contemporary primitive races.

Survival: The continued existence of the personality after the change or transition called death.

Sushupti: In Hindu metaphysical and occult philosophy, the highest form of separate consciousness, that of dreamless sleep.

Sutras: The second part of the Buddhist Tripitaka (q.v.), containing the teachings of Gautama Buddha. They consist of 250 chapters, divided in five *nikayas*.

Svabhava: Sanskrit for *innate disposition, essence, inherent or innate nature*. In the view of some Indian philosophers, the principle governing the universe through the spontaneity and individual character of the various substances. Other occultists regard it as the world-substance or its essence.

Swami: A Sanskrit word meaning spiritual preceptor, teacher, learned or holy man; used as an honorary title with proper names.

Swapna: In Hindu metaphysical and occult philosophy, the second-lowest degree of consciousness, that of dreaming, intermediate between the limitations of man's waking consciousness (*jagrat*) and the higher contemplation which is unlimited.

Swastika: A very ancient and widespread symbol, one of the most sacred and mystic diagrams in occultism, found both in the Eastern and Western hemispheres. It may be either right-hand (male) 卐 or left-hand (female) 卍; the former one is most generally used in India. In general it is regarded as the symbol of the sun; in India, especially, it is used as a symbol of good luck.

Sylph: An *elemental* (q.v.) of the element Air.

Symbolics: The study and interpretation of symbols.

Symbolism: Representation of an entity or idea in terms of another, usually the translation of an abstraction into concrete form.

Symbols, astrological: The planets, the signs of the Zodiac, and the aspects, are represented by certain symbols, understood by all astrologers. They are:

⊙ The Sun.
☽ The Moon.
☿ Mercury, related to the Caduceus.
♀ Venus.
⊕ The Earth.
♂ Mars, the shield and the spear of Ares.
♃ Jupiter.
♄ Saturn. The sickle of Chronos.
♅ Uranus, based on the H for Herschel.
♆ Neptune. The trident of the sea-god.
♇ Pluto.
☊ The Moon's North Node.   ☋ The Moon's South Node.
⊕ Fortuna. Since this symbol, commonly used for Fortuna, is the symbol for the Earth, some adaptation of the Moon symbol is recommended, in that Fortuna duplicates in a geoarc Figure the Moon's House position in a solar figure.

Signs of the Zodiac

Aries	♈︎		Libra	♎︎
Taurus	♉︎		Scorpio	♏︎
Gemini	♊︎		Sagittarius	♐︎
Cancer	⊗		Capricorn	♑︎
Leo	♌︎		Aquarius	♒︎
Virgo	♍︎		Pisces	♓︎

Aspects

Conjunction	0°	☌	Trine	120°	△
Semi-sextile	30°	⋎	Sesquiquadrate	135°	⍁
Semi-square	45°	>	Quincunx	150°	⅄
Sextile	60°	✳	Opposition	180°	☍
Square	90°	☐			

Elements:

Earth	⊕		Water	▽
Fire	△		Air	▬

Qualities:

Cardinal	∧	Fixed	▣	Mutable	⌒

Houses:

Angular	Γ		Ascendant	Asc.
Succedent	⊏		Descendant	Desc.
Cadent	L		Midheaven	MC
			Imum Coeli	IC

Sympathetic magic: Magic based on the principle of "like produces like," i.e., that things which resemble each other in shape or qualities have an occult affinity, and that certain relations between persons or things continue even after the relations have actually ceased to exist.

Sympathy: Reacting to the experiences and stimuli of another as if they were one's own; the sharing of emotions and interests.

Syzygy: A term literally meaning *yoking together*, often loosely applied in astrology to any conjunction or opposition; particularly of a planet with the Sun, and close to the ecliptic whereby the Earth and the two bodies are in a sight line. In its use in connection with the calculation of Tide Tables it applies to the conjunctions and oppositions of Sun and Moon near the Node.

T

Table-tilting, table-tipping: See: *Table-turning.*

Tablet of the Soul: A wooden tablet used in Chinese royal funerals; the name of the deceased was inscribed on it.

Table-turning: The simplest form of communicating with the spirits of the dead, using a table as the instrument of communication; the medium or all those present at the seance place their hands or fingertips on the table, which eventually begins to move and by pointing a leg at letters on a board on the floor, or by rapping according to a code, spells out the messages.

Taboo; tabu: A prohibition of a religious or magical nature. The word is derived from the Polynesian word *tabu,* meaning *forbidden.*

T'ai chi: In Chinese mysticism, the Great Ultimate.

T'ai ch'u: In Chinese mysticism, the "great beginning," interpreted as the primal condition when "there was non-being which had neither being nor name" and as the origin of the vital force (*ch'i*).

T'ai ho: Chinese for *Grand Harmony* or *Infinite Harmony,* the state and totality of being anterior to, but inclusive of, the Ultimate Vacuity (*t'ai hsu*) and the vital force (*ch'i*); identical with the One (*I*) or the Great Ultimate (*t'ai chi*).

T'ai hsu: Chinese for the *Ultimate Vacuity,* the course, the basis and the being of the material principle or the universal vital force (*ch'i*), the concentration and extension of which is to the Ultimate Vacuity as ice is to water.

T'ai hsuan: Chinese for the *Supremely Profound Principle,* "extending to and covering the myriad things without assuming any physical form, which created the universe by drawing its support from the Void, embraces the divinities, and determines the course of events." (Yang Hsiung, first century B.C.).

T'ai i: Chinese for the *Great Indeterminate*, the state of existence before the emergence of the vital force (*ch'i*). The *Ultimate Oneness*, which involves both Being (*yu*) and Non-Being (*wu*), and "which pervades Heaven and Earth, indeterminate but simple, existing but uncreated." (See also *ta i*.)

Ta i: In ancient Confucianism, the Great Unit, the Prime Force before the appearance of Heaven and Earth.

Ta shun: Chinese for *complete harmony*, as a result of the Profound Virtue or mysterious power.

Ta t'i: A Chinese term which in the teachings of Mencius means "that part of man which is great."

T'ai shih: Chinese for the *Great Beginning*, the first appearance of material form.

T'ai su: Chinese for the *Great Element*, the beginning of qualities of things.

Talisman: An object regarded capable of giving its owner or wearer superhuman powers, or of bestowing upon him other benefits and advantages. The talisman owes its efficacy to a property transmitted from without.

Talmud: An encyclopedic work in Hebrew-Aramaic produced during 800 years (300 B.C.-500 A.D.) in Palestine and Babylon. Its six Orders (*sedarim*), subdivided in sixty-three tractates (*massektoth*), sum up the oral traditions of Jewry, expounding, developing and commenting on the civil and religious laws of Judaism. It is a veritable treasure-house of ancient Jewish philosophy, ethics, theology, folklore, sciences, etc. accumulated during those eight centuries. The Talmud consists of an older part, the *Mishnah* (q.v.), and the later part, *Gemarah* (q.v.), a commentary on the former.

Tamas: One of the three constituents (*gunas*) of the Cosmic Substance (*prakriti*), viz. the restraining aspect of Nature that obstructs and envelops the other two constituents by counteracting the tendency of *rajas* to do work and *sattva* to reveal; in Yoga, the quality of delusion or ignorance.

Tanha: In Buddhist terminology, the will to lead a separate, personal incarnate existence.

Tanmatras: A Sanskrit term for the "subtle elements." There are five *tanmatras*, each *tanmatra* being the essence of one of the five basic elements (air, fire, earth, water and ether), viz. the essence of sound (*sabda*), touch (*sparsa*), form (*rupa*), flavor (*rasa*), and odor (*gandha*); they are the subtle objects of the sense powers (*indriyas*), the subtlest form of actual matter, without magnitude, supersensible, and perceived mediately only through gross objects.

Tantra: That body of Hindu religious literature which is stated to have been revealed by Shiva as the specific scripture of the *Kali Yuga* (the present age). The Tantras were the encyclopedias of esoteric knowledge of their time; the topics of a Tantra are: the creation of the universe, worship of the gods, spiritual exercise, rituals, the six magical powers, and meditation.

Tantric: Relating to or based on the Tantras (q.v.).

Tao: In Chinese philosophy, the Absolute—both the path and the goal. It denotes also the cosmic order, nature, and the Way in the cosmic sense, signifying that which is above the realm of corporeality.

Tao chiao: The Chinese name of Taoism (q.v.).

Tao shu: A Chinese term for the essence of Tao, or the axis of Tao at the center of which all Infinities converge and all distinctions disappear.

Taoism: The Chinese religion founded on the esoteric interpretation of the teachings of the Yellow Emperor and Lao Tzu, which assimilated the *yin-yang* philosophy (see *yin*), the practice of alchemy, and the worship of natural objects and immortals, and which became highly elaborated through the incorporation of a great many elements of Buddhism.

Tapas: Sanskrit for austerity, penance, meditation, intense application of Yoga.

Tarnkappe: In Teutonic myths, the cap which gives invisibility to the wearer.

Tarot: A deck of playing cards, based on a system of occult symbols arranged in a pattern of 78 cards; 22 of these are tarot cards ("major arcana"), the other 56 are suit cards ("minor arcana"). These cards can be used for divination. The term *tarot* is applied also to designate such divination.

Tashi Lama: The spiritual head of Lamaism (q.v.).

Tashlikh: The Hebrew mystical ceremony of the *casting off of sins* (q.v.).

Tat: An ancient Egyptian magic symbol, shaped $+$.

Tat tvam asi: Sanskrit for *that art thou,* the sum and substance of the instruction which Svetaketu received from his father according to the Chandogya Upanishad. The phrase is an allusion to the identity of the self with the essence of the world as the real.

Tattva: A Sanskrit term, literally meaning *thatness* or *whatness;* one of the principles ranging from abstract factors of conscious life to relations and laws governing natural facts. The Trika (q.v.) knows 36 *tattvas* which come into play when the universe "unfolds," i.e., is created by Shiva in an act variously symbolized by the awakening of his mind, or a "shining forth" (see *abhasa*).

Tariqat: The Moslem term for the path to mystic union with God.

Tau cross: A cross shaped like a capital T. Used by the Phoenicians as a magic symbol.

Taurus (The Bull): The second sign of the zodiac. Its symbol (♉) represents the head and horns of a bull. The sacred Apis was presumed to be the incarnation of the god Osiris—hence a symbol of a sepulchre or tomb. The Sun's entry into Taurus was celebrated as a Feast of Maya (Maia)—our May Day—the Sun represented by a white bull with a golden disc between his horns, followed by a procession of virgins, exemplifying the fecundity of Nature in Spring. The Sun is in Taurus annually from April 21 to May 20. Astrologically it is in the second thirty-degree arc from the Spring Equinox, from 30° to 60° along the Ecliptic. It is the "fixed" quality of the element Earth, conferring external will power that, ordinarily passive, and negative, becomes obstinate and unbending when aroused. Negative, nocturnal, cold, dry and melancholy. Ruler: Venus. Exaltation: Moon. Detriment: Mars. Fall: Uranus. Symbolic interpretation. The head and horns of a bull; the sacred Apis in whom the god Osiris was incarnate; a sepulchre or tomb.

Taurus era: See: *Cosmic epochs.*

Teacup reading: Divination by interpreting the shapes and relative positions assumed by tea leaves left on the bottom of a cup.

Telegnosis: Knowledge of another mind which is presumably not mediated by the perception of his body nor by any other physical influence by which communication between minds is ordinarily mediated. (Cf. *Telepathy.*)

Telekinesis: The moving faculty or practice of material objects by thought, without physical contact and without a perceptible means or agency.

Teleology: In general, the theory of the purpose, ends, goals, final causes and values of the Good. In metaphysics, the doctrine that reality is ordered by goals, ends, purposes, values, formal or final causes.

Telepathy. Transmissions of thoughts from one to another of two minds that presumably are in attunement or affinity, without the aid of any orthodox means of communication through ordinary channels of sensation. Defined in *The Journal of Parapsychology* as "extrasensory perception of the mental activities of another person. It does not include the clairvoyant perception of objective events."

Teleplasm: *Ectoplasm* (q.v.), acting at a distance from the body of the medium.

Telesm: An amulet, charm, or any other object worn to ward off evil.

Telesterion: The temple of Demeter where initiations in the Eleusinian mysteries were held.

Telesthesia: A limited form of clairvoyance, consisting in the perception of distant objects or conditions.

Telete: Initiation into the mysteries (q.v.) of ancient Greece.

Templars: The military order of the Knights Templar, founded in 1119 to protect pilgrims voyaging to Jerusalem. The order soon developed into a religious chivalry and acquired great wealth and power. In the 14th century, they were accused of heresy, black magic and Satanism and were persecuted and dissolved by the Church and temporal authorities.

Temple: Any place or edifice dedicated to the worship of deity or regarded as the dwelling place of deity. Also, the meeting place of esoteric or mystic fraternal orders, where their secret rituals are carried out.

Temple of the flesh: The physical body.

Tendai: The Japanese "Pure Land" sect of Buddhism, which regards Amitabha the greatest of all Buddhas and centers its doctrine around him.

Tengus: Evil tree spirits (Japan), human in form but hatched from eggs.

Tephromancy: Divination by writing in ashes.

Tepitoton: Small household deities of ancient Mexico.

Testimony: The term preferred by the Society of Friends (Quakers) to designate a principle or tenet of faith, as the Friends (Quakers) are opposed to "doctrine." The Quaker Testimonies include Plainness of Speech, Refusal of the Oath, Plainness of Dress, Testimony against War, etc.

Tetrabiblos (Greek for *Four Books*): An encyclopedia of astrology, said to be the record of the oldest astrological systems. It dates from about 132-160 A.D. In it the author, Claudius Ptolemy, the great Egyptian mathematician, says that it was compiled from "ancient" sources.

Tetractys: The "perfect number" of the Pythagoreans and of the numerologists, composed of the Divine monad (One), the dyad (Two), the primeval triad (Three) and the fundamental sacred tetrad (Four). The symbol of the tetractys, originated by Pythagoras, consists of ten dots arranged in four rows above each other (four dots in the bottom line, three dots in the one above them, two in the next line, and a single dot on top), forming an equilateral triangle. In occultism, this diagram is also referred to as *tetractys* and is believed to have very great occult, mystic power and significance.

Tetrad: In numerology, the number Four.

Tetragram: A magic diagram (q.v.), consisting of a four-pointed star formed by interlacing two columns or pillars. Symbolic of the four elements, it has been used for conjuring the elementary spirits.

Tetragrammaton: Greek for *four-letter unit*. A Kabalistical term for the Hebrew name of God, which consists of the four Hebrew letters *Yod, He, Vov, He* (*J-H-V-H* or *I-H-V-H*).

Tezcatlipoca: Warrior god of the Aztecs, punisher of evil-doers, god of the waning moon; a counterpart of the god Quetzalcoatl.

Thaumaturgist: A miracle-worker.

Thaumaturgy: The power or art of "working wonders" with divine or other superhuman aid.

Theism: In general, that type of religion or religious philosophy which incorporates a conception of God as a unitary being, thus may be considered equivalent to monotheism.

Theistic personalism: The theory that God is the ground of all being, immanent in and transcendent over the whole world of reality. It is pan-psychic but avoids pantheism by asserting the complementary nature of immanence and transcendance which come together in and are in some degree essential to all personality. This term used for the modern form of theism.

Theogony: The study and theory of the origin and genealogy of the various deities.

Theology: The study of the question of God and the relation of God to the world of reality.

Theomachy: Battle against the gods; opposition to the divine will.

Theomancy: The general meaning of the word is: Divination by oracles considered to be divinely inspired. The term is used also as the name of that part of the Hebrew Kabalah devoted to the study of the Majesty of God and to the mastery of the sacred names believed to be the key to the power of divination and magical ability.

Theopathy: Religious fanaticism.

Theophagy: Literally, *eating the god*. The practice, found in a great many primitive religions and in the esoteric mysteries ("mystery religious"), of eating the flesh of a sacrifice or sacred animal in whose flesh the god is believed to dwell, in order to absorb supernatural power.

Theophany: The manifestation of a god to man by actual appearance.

Theopneusty: Divine inspiration.

Theosophical Society: The Theosophical Society, or "Universal Brotherhood," was founded in New York, in 1875, by Col. H. S. Olcott and H. P. Blavatsky, helped by W. O. Judge and several others. According to *The Theosophical Glossary* (by H. P. Blavatsky), "its avowed object was at first the specific investigation of psychic or so-called 'spiritualistic' phenomena, after which its three chief objects were declared, namely (1) Brotherhood of man, without distinction of race, colour, religion or social position; (2) the serious study of the ancient world-religions for purposes of comparison and the selection therefrom of universal ethics; (3) the study and development of the latent *divine* powers in man."

Theosophy: In general, a philosophical system claiming to be divine wisdom and the true knowledge of the existence and nature of the deity. Specifically, the word is used to designate the "wisdom-religion" propagated by the Theosophical Society (q.v.).

Theurgic mirror: A bottle of clear water, in which pictures appear before the eyes of a child gazing into the water, in reply to questions asked by him.

Theurgy: The literal meaning of this Greek term is *divine work*, and it is generally applied to denote the work of a divine or other supernatural agency in the affairs of man, generally by direct intervention. In occult terminology, it means communication with supernatural beings and the practice of magic rites aimed at bringing Gods and spirits down to the Earth.

Thiasoi: Brotherhoods of the adherents of the initiates of the Orphic mysteries.

Third eye: That organ which is considered to enable a living human being to see the astral world. Identified by occultists with the glandlike appendage of the brain called the pineal body.

Thor: Thunder-god of Norse mythology, a god of fertility and agriculture, patron of sailors.

Thoth: Ibis-headed god of ancient Egypt, god of wisdom, and magical arts, inventor of writing, patron of literature.

Thought form: In occult terminology, a form or shape which the imagination of an adept or medium has constructed out of cosmic matter in the visible world and materializes in that same visible world.

Thought-reading: See: *Mind reading.*

Thought-transference: The former term for *telepathy* (q.v.).

Three Plenties: See: *Fu lu shou.*

Three Stars: See: *Fu lu shou.*

Thumoni: A Burmese shamanistic medium or tribal medicine-man.

Thundering rod: In the literature on occultism and black magic, this term is frequently used to designate the magic wand of the sorcerer. (Also called *thundering wand* or *blasting rod*.)

Thurifumia: Divination by the use of the smoke of incense as source of divinatory omens.

Ti: This Chinese term has three meanings: (*a*) The Confucian anthropomorphic Lord or Supreme Lord (Shang To), almost interchangeable with Heaven (T'ien) except that Ti refers to the Lord as the directing and governing power whereas Heaven refers to the Lord in the sense of omnipresence and all-inclusiveness. (*b*) The world-honored deities (such as those of the four directions and the Five Elements). (*c*) Mythological sovereigns whose virtues approximate those of Heaven and Earth.

Tiamat: In Babylonian and Chaldean cosmogony, the undifferentiated matter out of which gods and men, heaven and earth sprang.

T'ien jen: Chinese for *heavenly man*, understood as a human being "who is not separated from The Natural." (Taoism)

Tii: The Polynesian name of the *vampire* (q.v.).

Time: The general medium in which all events take place in succession or appear to take place in succession. All specific and finite periods of time, whether past, present or future, constitute merely parts of the entire and single Time. (Cf. *time track, space-time*.)

Time-perception: The apprehension of the protensive or durational character of the data of experience.

Time track: According to many esoteric philosophers and occultists, time sequence—past, present and future—is just a human concept; time is indivisible, externally extant, and past, present and future are merely concepts of the human mind which moves along a "time track" on a one-way trip through the reality which is time. Adherents to this view explain prescience, premonitions, prophecy, etc. as glimpses ahead along the time track.

Timeless: Having no end in time, pertaining to no time, or transcending time.

Tisiphone: One of the three Furies (q.v.).

Titans: The giants of Greek mythology who made war on the gods.

Tohunga: Tribal priest-mediums of the Maoris of New Zealand.

Totem: An animal regarded by savage or primitive races as the carrier or abode of the soul of a deceased person. (See *totemism.*)

Totemism: Belief in totems and totemistic relationships. A feature of primitive social organizations whereby the members of a tribe possess group solidarity by virtue of their association with a class of animals or in some cases plants or inanimate objects.

Tradition: The total body of accepted group beliefs; the nonmaterial content of the cultural heritage of a nation, race or other group transmitted continuously from generation to generation.

Traducianism: The view, dating back to Tertullian (200 A.D.), that the soul (as well as the body) is generated from the souls of the parents—that the process of natural propagation procreates the soul.

Trance: A state of apparent unconsciousness, in which the body is susceptible to possession. A trance may be spontaneous or induced (as in hypnotism). Specifically, the mediumistic trance, in which a medium communicates with the astral forms or spirits of the deceased.

Transataumancy: Divination on the basis of omens seen unexpectedly.

Transcendental hearing. *Clairaudience* (q.v.).

Transcendental vision: *Clairvoyance* (q.v.).

Transfiguration: The ability of a medium to assume bodily characteristics of deceased person.

Transition: A Rosicrucian term for "physical death."

Transitor: In astrological terminology, a slow-moving major planet whose lingering aspect to a birth planet produces a displacement of equilibrium, which is then activated by an additional aspect from a Culminator, a faster-moving body such as the Sun or Moon, to the same or another planet, thereby precipitating the externalization.

Transmigration of the soul: The rebirth of the soul, the personality, in a new body—human, animal, even plant, demonic or divine. (Cf. *reincarnation.*)

Transmutation: In astrological terminology, the advantageous utilization, on the part of a controlled and developed character, of an astrological influence which otherwise might exert a destructive and disruptive force.

Transmutation of metals: The goal of the alchemists; especially the transmutation of mercury or other baser elements into gold.

Transmutation of the body: The supreme goal of alchemy, the restoration of man to the state of beauty, perfection and physical immortality.

Transport: An ecstatic moment of high spiritual experience.

Travellers' ring: A magic ring said to enable the wearer to travel long distances without tiring.

Tree marriage: A ceremony, practiced in parts of India, symbolically uniting a man or woman in marriage to a tree; it is sometimes a part of the wedding ritual, sometimes it is a mystic ritual which enables a younger brother or sister to marry before an elder one.

Tree of life: See: *Etz Hayim.*

Tretya yuga: The Sanskrit name of the second age (*yuga*) of the *manvantara;* it is one-fourth less righteous and briefer than the preceding one, enduring 1,296,000 of our years (three-tenths of the entire *manvantara*).

Triad: A divine trinity or group or union of three gods, e.g., Brahma, Vishnu and Shiva. (See also *higher triad.*)

Triad: In numerology, the number Three.

Tribal god: A deity worshiped by and considered as the patron of a particular tribe.

Trichotomy: Literally, *division into three parts.* Specifically, in theology, the doctrine that man consists of soul, spirit and body. In occultism, the term is often applied also to any view involving or concerning a *triad* (q.v.).

Trigram: See: *Pa kua.*

Trika: An Indian philosophic system founded by Vasugupta in the 9th cent. A.D., having flourished among the Shaivites of Kashmir till the 14th cent., and now reviving. Its aim is the recognition of Shiva as one's own inmost nature from which ensues progressive dissolution of manifoldness and reduction of the threefold reality of Shiva, *sakti* (q.v.), and soul to Oneness, thus reversing the "unfolding" of the universe through the 36 *tattvas* (q.v.).

Trikaya: Sanskrit for *triple body*. That school in Buddhist mysticism which conceives of the Buddha as having three bodies, viz.: The Law-Body (*Dharma-kaya*) which is the soul of Buddha, the Enjoyment-Body (*Sambhogakaya*) which is the embodiment of Wisdom, and the Transformation-Body (*Nirmana-kaya*) which is the embodiment of compassion.

Trimurti: The Hindu triad of gods: Brahma, the creator, Vishnu, the preserver, and Shiva, the destroyer.

Trine: In astrology, an aspect of 120 degrees.

Trinities: See: *Signs*.

Tripitaka: "The Three Baskets," the Buddhistic Canon as finally adopted by the Council of Sthaviras, or elders, held under the auspices of Emperor Asoka, about 245 B.C., at Pataliputra, consisting of three parts: "The basket of discipline" (*Vinaya*), "the basket of (Buddha's) sermons" (*Sutras*), and "the basket of metaphysics" (*Abidharma*).

Triton: In Greek mythology, a merman, son of Poseidon and Amphitrite.

Troll: A hideous, evil earth-demon of Teutonic mythology, living in caves.

Ts'ai: Chinese for *power*. In Chinese mysticism, Heaven, Earth and Man are referred to as the three powers or forces of Nature.

T.·.S.·.G.·.A.·.O.·.T.·.U.·.: The logogram used by Freemasons for *The Sovereign Grand Architect of the Universe*, the Masonic name of the Deity.

Tso wang: Chinese for "sitting in forgetfulness"; that state of absolute freedom, in which the distinctions between others and self is forgotten, in which life and death are equated, in which all things have become one. A state of pure experience, in which one becomes at one with the infinite soul.

Tsao hua: A Chinese term for Heaven and Earth; the Active or Male Cosmic Principle (*yang*) and the Passive or Female Cosmic Principle (*yin*). Also used as a synonym for *tsao wu* (*che*), meaning Creator.

Tsao wu (che): Chinese for *Creator*. (Also called *tsao hua*.)

Ts'un hsing: A Chinese term, the meaning of which is: putting the desires into proper harmony by restraint; the way to achieve "complete preservation of one's nature."

Tu: Lao Tzu's term for "steadfastness in quietude," in order to comprehend Fate, The Eternal, and Tao.

T'u: Chinese for *Earth*, one of the five Elements or Agents in Chinese mystic philosophy. (See *wu hsing*.)

Tu hua: This Chinese term means spontaneous transformation, the universal law of existence, the guiding principle of which is neither any divine agency nor any moral law but Tao.

Tuat: The underworld, abode of the dead, in Egyptian myths.

Tuatha de Danaan: In ancient Irish mythology, gods living underground. (The name literally means *the folk of the goddess Danu*.)

Tutelary god: A religious entity or power serving as a guardian or protector of an individual, family, tribe, city or nation.

Twilight of the gods: In Norse mythology, the final battle between the gods and their enemies, the evil giants.

Twins: See: *Gemini.*

Two-factor religion: A term coined by F. L. Parrish, to designate any religion in which all religious ideas and practices of faith are based on the assumption that the religious factor (q.v.) native to man and that native to non-human nature powers are different and mutually exclusive factors; the religions which assume that there are two impinging worlds—the human world of the here and hereafter, and the world of the immortals (gods, demons and spirits).

Typtology: Communication with the spirits of the departed or other discarnate entities by means of rappings interpreted according to prearranged codes.

Tzaddik: The leader of a community of *Hassidim.*

Tzadkiel: In Jewish mysticism, the angel of benevolence, grace, piety and justice.

Tzu hua: A Taoist term for self-transformation or spontaneous transformation without depending on any divine guidance or external agency, but following the thing's own principle of being, which is Tao.

U

Uma. A gentle, kind Hindu goddess, consort of Shiva.

Umbra: Latin for *shadow*. In occultism, the astral body or etheric double (q.v.) which lingers about the tomb of the physical body after the death of the latter, kept there by attraction impressed on physical matter by the emanations of the body in its lifetime in the material world.

Umbratiles: In mediumistic terminology, astral appearances which may become visible and occasionally tangible, too, by attracting material elements from the body of a medium or from the surrounding atmosphere.

Unanimism: A term invented by Jules Romains to mean (1) a belief "in a certain reality of a spiritual nature," and (2) a belief that the human soul can enter into direct, immediate, and intuitive communication with the universal soul.

Unconscious mind: A compartment of the mind which lies outside the consciousness.

Undine: An *elemental* (q.v.) of the element Water; undines are believed to appear usually in the shapes of women, but able also to assume the forms of fishes or snakes.

Unio mystica: Latin for *mystic union*. (See: *Union*.)

Union: The *mystic union* is the state in which the Self merges into the Absolute Life, and becomes one with it.

Universal balm: A synonym for the *elixir of life* (q.v.).

Universal Brotherhood: See: *Theosophical Society*.

Universal mind: The consciousness of the Supreme Being, which pervades and permeates the entire universe. (See also: *World Soul*.)

Universal solvent: In the terminology of alchemy, the substance which will resolve every composite body into the homogeneous substance from which they evolved; it also rejuvenates man's body, makes it immune to disease and prolongs life.

Universal Spirit: See: *Universal Mind.*

Universe: The complete natural world.

Unmesha: Sanskrit for *becoming visible.* The manifestation or creation of the universe.

Upadhi: Sanskrit for *substitute, disguise.* One of many conditions of body and mind obscuring the true state of man or his self which Indian philosophies try to remove for the attainment of *moksha* (q.v.). In occult terminology, this word is used in the sense of a "carrier of something lighter or subtler than itself"— for instance, the body is the *upadhi* of the spirit.

Upanishad: Sanskrit for *secret teaching* or *Esoteric Doctrine.* The Upanishads form the third section of the Vedas, recording the speculations of the Hindu sages and esoteric adepts on the nature of the world and ultimate reality and the way to spiritual union with The Absolute. The principal basis of Hindu philosophy. More than one hundred Upanishads are mentioned, but thirteen are generally listed as the oldest ones, viz. *Chandogya, Brhadaranyaka, Aitareya, Taittiriya, Katha, Isa, Munda, Kausitaki, Kena, Prasna, Svetasvatara, Mandukya,* and *Maitri;* they probably date from the 8th century B.C.

Uranian Astrology: A system based upon the teachings of Alfred Witte of the Hamburg (Germany) Astrology School. Its chief differences from the orthodox school consist in the use of Planetary Patterns based upon Midpoints, the cardinal points, Antiscions, and certain hypothetical planets; also the exclusion of all but the "hard" angles: conjunction, semi-square, quadrate, sesquiquadrate and opposition—which are termed effective connections. The personal points are 0° Aries, Cancer, Libra and Capricorn, Ascendant, Midheaven, Sun and Moon.

Urim and Thummim: Objects attached to the breastplate of the High Priest of the ancient Hebrews and used by him as accessories for divination, to learn the will of God on questions of great national importance.

Ushabtiu: A little figurine or statuette, a number of which were entombed with the body of each deceased in ancient Egypt; the duty of the *ushabtiu* was to answer for the deceased during the trial of judgment before the divine judges, and to cultivate the fields for the deceased in the next world. (Also referred to as *ushabti*.)

Utmost Invincibility, Stage of: See: *Dasa-bhumi*.

Utu: The Sumerian god of the sun and of justice.

Vac: Sanskrit for *speech, voice, word.* In Vedic and occult philosophy *vac* has a similar role as the *Logos* in Greek philosophy. It appears personified as the goddess of speech and close to primeval reality in the hierarchy of emanations.

Vahana: Sanskrit for *vehicle* (q.v.).

Vaishesika: The Hindu philosophical system which teaches that knowledge of the nature of reality is obtained by knowing the special properties or essential differences which distinguish the nine Eternal Realities or Substances: Earth, Water, Fire, Air, Ether, Time, Space, Self, and Mind.

Vaishnavism: See: *Vishnuism.*

Vala: A Teutonic and Scandinavian term for *seeress.*

Valhalla: The "hall of the blessed heroes" of Norse mythology, the abode of the brave warriors slain in battle.

Valkyries: In Norse mythology, female superhuman entities, who take the souls of the slain to the Valhalla and before Odin.

Vampire: The designation of an astral form which lives by drawing vitality and strength from living humans. According to occultists, a vampire may be the astral body of a person still living or that of a dead and buried body to which it still clings and which it tries to nourish and thus to prolong its own existence.

Vampirization: In occultism, parasitic preying on another person's energy and vitality.

Vanir: In Norse mythology, a group of gods who dwell in Vanaheim; deities of wealth, commerce, fruitfulness, antagonists of Odin and his group of gods.

Varuna: The all-seeing Vedic sky god, god of law and order in the world.

Vasanas: In Hindu mystic and occultistic terminology, the tendencies inherent but latent in a man as residues from a previous incarnation and affecting his actions in his present life.

Vasudeva: In Hinduism, the father of Krishna.

Vaulderie: A term used by the officials of the Inquisition for the crime of black magic and Satanism.

Veda: The generic name for the most ancient sacred literature of the Hindus, consisting of the four collections called (1) *Rig Veda*, hymns to gods, (2) *Sama Veda*, priests' chants, (3) *Yajur Veda*, sacrificial formulae in prose, and (4) *Atharva Veda*, magical chants; each Veda is divided into two broad divisions, viz. (1) *Mantra*, hymns, and (2) *Brahmana*, precepts, which include (a) *Aranyakas*, theology, and (b) *Upanishads*, philosophy; the Vedas are classified as *revealed literature;* they contain the first philosophical insights and are regarded as the final authority; tradition makes *Vyasa* the compiler and arranger of the Vedas in their present form; the Vedic period is conservatively estimated to have begun about 1500 to 1000 B.C.

Vedanta: The best known and most popular formulation of Hindu mystic philosophy, which teaches that the phenomenal world is mere illusion and has only seeming reality, as have also the apparent individual selves of the world, and there is but one self, Brahman-Atman; he who knows "that, soul art thou," attains *moksha* and is released from the wheel of existence.

Vedic: An adjective, meaning referring to the Vedas (q.v.) or the period that generated them, considered closed about 500 B.C.

Vedic Hinduism: The religion and philosophy of the Vedas. It is basically optimistic and life-loving. The four Vedas and the Atharva-Veda are the literature of this period which later changed into Brahmanic Hinduism (q.v.).

Vendidad: A Zoroastrian priestly code, which gives detailed instructions regarding purification, punishments and techniques of expiation, also instructions for protective magic.

Venus: The Italic goddess of gardens who was later identified with the Greek Aphrodite as the goddess of beauty.

Verbum mentis: Latin for *mental word* (q.v.).

Verdelet: According to demonographers, the demon whose duties include the transportation of the witches to the Witches' Sabbath.

Vestal Virgins: Guardians of the sacred perpetual fire in the temple of Vesta, chief Roman household divinity; they were believed to have magic powers.

Via mystica: Latin for *mystic way.* The way to mystic union with God.

Vibhuta: Sanskrit for "manifestation of great power." In Yoga, the eight supernatural, mystic powers which one can attain, viz. (1) the power of becoming as minute as an atom, (2) the power to become as light as cotton, (3) the power of reaching anywhere, even to the moon, (4) the power of having all wishes of whatever description realized, (5) the power to expand oneself into space, (6) the power to create, (7) the power to command all, and (8) the power of suppressing all desires.

Vibrations: In occultism, a psychic pulsation or magnetic waves.

Vidhi: Sanskrit for rule, formula, sacred precept or scripture.

Vidya: Sanskrit for *knowledge.* In theosophy, the "wisdom knowledge" which enables man to distinguish between true and false.

Vijnana: Sanskrit for *consciousness;* the faculty of apprehension or individualization of experience, and as such perhaps equivalent to *ahamkara* (q.v.); intellectual, not intuitional, knowledge.

Vijnana-vada: Sanskrit for *theory of consciousness;* specifically that consciousness is of the essence of reality; also the Buddhist school of subjective idealism otherwise known as Yogacara (q.v.).

Vinaya: The first part of the Buddhist *Tripitaka,* containing the code of rules governing the lives of monks, whether alone or in communities.

Virgin: See: *Virgo.*

Virgo (The Virgin): The sixth sign of the zodiac. Its symbol (♍) is probably a representation of the Girdle of Hymen, and has reference to the Immaculate Conception of a Messiah. It is usually pictured by a virgin holding in her hand a green branch, an ear of corn, or a spike of grain. Spica is a star in the constellation of Virgo. Here was commemorated the Festival of Ishtar, goddess of fertility. The Sun is in Virgo annually from August 23 to September 22. Astrologically and astronomically it is the thirty-degree arc immediately preceding the Sun's passing over the Fall

Equinoctial point, occupying a position along the Ecliptic from 150° to 180°. It is the "mutable" quality of the element Earth: negative, cold, dry, sterile, human; also critical, practical, helpful. Ruler: Mercury. Detriment: Jupiter. Fall: Venus. Symbolic interpretation: A green branch, an ear of wheat or corn; the Immaculate Virgin who gives birth to a world-savior.

Vishnu: One of the three gods of the Hindu Trinity (Brahma, the Creator, Vishnu, the Preserver, and Shiva, the Destroyer), and as such he is one of the three aspects of Ishwara, the Personal God. To the adherents of *Vaishnavism*, Vishnu is the supreme deity.

Vishnuism: One of the three great divisions in modern Hinduism (the other two are *Shaivism and Shaktism*); its followers identify Vishnu—rather than Brahma and Shiva—with the Supreme Being, and are exclusively devoted to his worship, regarding him as the Creator, Preserver and Destroyer of the universe.

Vision: The appearance of supernatural entities or scenes to the eyes of mortals.

Vital body: The etheric double (q.v.).

Vital force: Cf. *Vitalism.*

Vital soul: Personalized vitality.

Vitalism: The doctrine that phenomena of life possess a character sui generis by virtue of which they differ radically from physico-chemical phenomena. The vitalist ascribes the activities of living organisms to the operation of a vital force.

Vlkodlak; vukodlak: The name of the werewolf (q.v.) in the Slavic countries of Eastern Europe.

Vohumanah: In Zoroastrianism, one of the six Amesha Spentas (q.v.), personified representation of good thought, spirit of the human race.

Volatile: The alchemical name of mercury. (*Fixed volatile* is the mercury remaining at the bottom of a vessel after the process of evaporation.)

Voodoo: Black magic or witchcraft of the West Indies.

Voyance: *Clairvoyance* (q.v.); loosely, psychometry and psi abilities in general.

Vulcan: An hypothetical planet of the solar system, the orbit of which is supposed to lie inside that of Mercury.

Vyapakatva: Sanskrit for *omnipresence, all-pervasiveness.*

Wai tan: The ancient Chinese school of alchemy and magic.

Wakan; wakanda: An American Indian (Sioux) term for a life-power which permeates all natural objects and forces; a natural but unusual power inherent in objects affecting all phases of man's life.

Wake: The keeping of a vigil or watch at the side of a corpse until the time of burial.

Warlock: A male witch. (Scotland)

Water Bearer: See: *Aquarius*.

Water-sprite: A nature-spirit of the water.

Weather god. A deity, found (under various names) in the mythology of many ancient and primitive races or tribes, believed to bestow fertility through rain.

Werabana: Evil spirits of Polynesian folklore.

Weretiger: The *jadi-jadian* of Malayan occult lore; a man who can change or has changed himself, or has been changed, into a tiger.

Werewolf: In occult lore, a man who can change himself or has changed himself or has been changed, temporarily or permanently, into a wolf.

Western Yoga: A designation sometimes applied to Theosophy, also to the New Thought movement and Christian Science, whose followers, however, seriously object to this name.

Wheel of life: (1) *Samsara* (q.v.)—(2) A wheel often depicted in Tibetan paintings, setting forth the basic beliefs in reincarnation found in Lamaism. The endless circumference of the wheel is symbolic of immortality; the three prominences of the hub symbolize the three great vices, ignorance, lust and anger, a lapse into which will make the wrongdoer reincarnate as an insect or other low life-form in his next life; the six spokes symbolize the six principle divisions of life and religion: the gods, the demi-gods, hell, the tortured souls, human beings, and animals.

Wheel of prayer: A small barrel-shaped device, made of a metal (often silver) or wood, used in Tibet. Written prayers to Buddha are stuffed into the hollow of the device. Each turn of the wheel is believed to repeat all the prayers inserted to Buddha again and again. (Large wheels of prayer are used for community purposes.)

White Magic: The use of supernormal powers and abilities self-lessly, for the benefit of others.

White sect of Lamaism: See: *Kagyud*.

White shaman: A shaman (q.v.) who claims to have relations with celestial deities and powers of the Good only.

White voodoo sect: That sect of the voodoo cult which coun-tenances only the sacrifice of white fowls and goats, but forbids human sacrifice.

Wild-women: Nature-spirits of German folklore.

Will-o'-the-wisp. *Ignis fatuus* (q.v.).

Wine of life: The wine which according to Jewish mystic tra-dition has been kept in Paradise for the pious since the creation of the world.

Wisdom religion: The secret doctrine (q.v.) on which all occult and esoteric teachings are based; theosophy.

Witch: A mortal woman who is a devoted servant of the in-fernal empire, who has supernatural powers and the ability to practice black magic.

Witchcraft: The art or practice of black magic or sorcery with the aid of evil spirits or familiars.

Witch-doctor: The magician or medicine-man of a primitive tribe, usually credited with the ability to detect witches and to exorcise evil demons.

Witches' ointment: The salve which according to medieval demonologists witches used to anoint themselves in order to be able to perform certain magical feats.

Witches' Sabbath: Reunions believed in the middle ages to be held by witches and sorcerers. (The *Great Sabbath* was supposed to be held once every three months, for all witches and sorcerers in a country; the *Little Sabbath* was supposed to be held weekly, for those in a town or a small region.)

Wizard: While the word is used commonly to mean a male witch, its proper meaning is: magician or sorcerer.

Wonder rabbi: In Jewish mystic lore, a Hasidistic rabbi of great mystic knowledge and magic powers.

World axis: See: *Axis mundi*.

World of action: See: *World of matter*.

World of emanations: According to Kabalistic teachings, the world of Adam Kadmon, the heavenly man, a direct emanation from the En Soph.

World era; world epoch: See: *Cosmic epochs*.

World of matter: According to Kabalistic teachings, the abode of evil spirits, divided into ten spheres or zones, the lowest of which represents the deepest state of evil; ruled by the evil spirit Sammael. (Also referred to as *world of action*.)

World-line: A line conceived in four dimensions; a line cutting across *space-time* (q.v.).

World-point: A four-dimensional point; a durationless geometrical point. (Cf. *space-time*.)

World Soul: In mysticism and occultism, an intelligent, animating, indwelling principle of the cosmos, its organizing and integrating cause, which permeates and animates everything in nature. According to occult teachings, all sentient life is fused, blended and unified by the World Soul, so that in reality there is no such thing as separateness. Oriental occultists call it *alaya;* the medieval mystic philosophers referred to it as *anima mundi*. (See also *akasha*.)

World substance: In esotericism, the substance of which the world is composed, the "plastic essence of matter," from which all nature issues forth and to which it returns at the end of the life-cycle.

World-Teacher: According to occult philosophy, an Elder Brother (q.v.), one of the three leaders of the Great White Lodge (q.v.); he is concerned, in his various incarnations at various periods of history, with spiritual and religious enlightenment and evolution.

Wotan; Wodan: The West Germanic forms of the name *Odin*.

Wraith: The *astral body* (q.v.) of a living person; the apparition of a wraith is generally regarded by occultists as a sign of death.

Wu: Chinese for *Eternal Non-Being;* that which is opposed to the being of material objects; refers to the essence of *Tao*, the first principle. (Lao Tzu.)

Wu: Chinese for creatures, things, matter, the material principle, the external world, the non-self, objects of the senses and desires, affairs.

Wu chi: Chinese for the *Non-Ultimate*.

Wu hsing: In Chinese, the five elements (Water, Fire, Wood, Metal and Earth) which give rise to the multiplicity of things and which have their correspondence in the five senses, tastes, colors, tones, the five virtues, the five atmospheric conditions, the five ancient emperors, etc. The term is used also for the Five Agents which are the five vital forces (*ch'i*) engendered by the transformation of *yang*, the active cosmic principle, and its union with *yin*, the passive cosmic principle, each with its specific nature.

Wu wu: In Chinese philosophy, the meaning of this term is: to regard things as things, that is, to regard things with objectivity and no attachment or selfishness, on the one hand, and, with the conviction that the self and the non-self form an organic unity on the other.

Xenoglossis: The speaking of a medium in languages unknown to him or in non-existent pseudo-languages.

Xibalba: The underworld of the religion of the Quiché Indians of Central America.

Xylomancy: Divination by interpreting the positions and shapes of dry twigs or other wood found on the ground.

Y

Y-Kim: A Chinese book on mysticism, believed to originate from the 35th century B.C.

Yajna: Sanskrit for *sacrifice*, a Vedic institution which became philosophically interpreted as the self-sacrifice of the Absolute One which, by an act of self-negation (*nisedha-vyapara*) became the Many.

Yajur Veda: One of the four Vedas, highly ritualistic in character.

Yakin: In Kabalistic and Masonic tradition, the red pillar of bronze cast for Solomon's temple; the symbol of Intelligence (*Binah*, the third of the *Sephiroth*—q.v.).

Yakshas: Evil demons of Hindu folklore.

Yama: Sanskrit for *moral restraint* or *self control* which is the first prerequisite to the study and practice of Yoga (q.v.); ten rules of conduct (*yamas*) are listed in the classic text, *Hathayogapradipika*, viz. non-injuring, truthfulness, non-stealing, continence, forgiveness, endurance, compassion, sincerity, sparing diet, and cleanliness.

Yama and Yami: In the Vedas, twin brother and sister who are the parents of the human race.

Yang: Chinese name of the active principle of the universe—the male, active force. In Neo-Confucianism, *yin* (q.v.) and *yang* constitute the vital force which is the material principle of the universe.

Yang ch'i: In Taoism, nourishing life through breath control. In Confucianism, nourishing one's vital force, the basis of the human body, by the practice of benevolence, righteousness, and uprightness, and the obedience of the moral law.

Yantra: A mystic diagram of occult powers, usually drawn on copper or other metal tablets. The power of yantras used in connection with appropriate *mantras* is irresistible according to occult teachings.

Yareah: Ancient Canaanite moon god.

Yashts: Avestan hymns of praise in honor of Zoroastrian divine beings.

Yasna: Zoroastrian liturgies in the Avesta, including invocations to Ahura-Mazda and other gods.

Yauhahu: A South American Indian word for a malignant spirit.

Yazatas: Nature-spirits or minor deities of Zoroastrianism.

Yekanta bhakti: In *bhakti yoga* (q.v.) the interior and silent adoration of the ineffable formless, ubiquitous Presence.

Yellow sect of Lamaism: See: *Gelug.*

Yesod: The Archetypal World of the Jewish Kabalistic mystic philosophers, in which the true or spirit forms of all things created exist. Many authors consider this Archetypal World to be the same as the *astral world* or *astral plane* of contemporary esoteric philosophy.

Yetzirah: According to Kabalistic teachings, the world of angels, formed from emanations of the Briah (q.v.). Also called *Yetziratic World. Yetzirah* is also the title of the most occult of Kabbalistic books (*Sepher Yetzirah*).

Yezidi: A mystic religious community in Kurdistan, numbering about 20,000. Although *Yezidi* means "Worshipper of God," they are usually called *Devil Worshippers.* They regard themselves as descendants of Adam alone and isolate themselves strictly from the rest of mankind, descendants of Adam and Eve.

Yggdrasil: The world-tree of Norse mythology, whose leaves are always green. Fire will destroy it in the twilight of the gods.

Yi: Chinese for *change,* a fundamental principle of the universe, arising out of the interaction of the two cosmic forces of *yin* and *yang,* or passive and active principles, and manifested in natural phenomena, human affairs, and ideas. (Also spelled *i.*)

Yi King: See: *Book of Changes.*

Yin: Chinese name of the passive principle of the universe—the female, negative force. In Neo-Confucianism, *yin* and *yang* (q.v.) constitute the vital force which is the material principle of the universe.

Yoga: Sanskrit for *union*. The development of the powers latent in man for achieving union with the Divine Spirit. It is defined as "the restraint of mental modifications." Eight stages are enumerated, viz. moral restraint (*yama*), self-culture (*niyama*), posture (*asana*) breath-control (*pranayama*), control of the senses (*pratyahara*), concentration (*dharana*), meditation (*dhyana*), and a state of superconsciousness (*samadhi*). The techniques of Yoga are recognized and applied by all schools of occultism.

Yogacara: A Mahayana Buddhist school which puts emphasis on Yoga as well as *acara*, ethical conduct.

Yogasutras: Famous work by Patanjali, on which Yoga is founded. It is essentially a mental discipline in eight stages (see: *Yoga*) for the attainment of spiritual freedom without neglecting physical and moral preparation.

Yogin: A follower of or adept in *yoga*.

Yomi: In Japanese occultism, the spirit world or astral world.

Yu. Chinese for *eternal being*, referring to the function of the metaphysical principle Tao; it is no mere zero or nothingness, having as the first principle brought all things into being.

Yuan: Chinese for *beginning*. In mysticism and occult philosophy, this term has several meanings: (*a*) the beginning of the material principle or the vital force (*ch'i*); (*b*) the originating power of the Heavenly Element (*chien*) in the system of the Eight Elements (*pa kua*); (*c*) One, the beginning of number; (*d*) the great virtue of Heaven and Earth which expresses itself in production and reproduction. (See also: *i yuan*.)

Yuan ch'i: Chinese for *primal fluid*, or the Prime-Force, the product of the cosmos. Its pure and light portion collected to form Heaven and its impure and heavy portion, Earth.

Yuga: One of the four ages of the world, viz. the *Satya yuga*, (the golden age) the *tretya yuga*, the *dwapara yuga* and the *kali yuga* (the dark age). The first three have already elapsed and we are now living in the last which began at midnight between the 17th and 18th of February 3102 B.C. The duration of each age is said to be, respectively, 1,728,000, 1,296,000, 864,000, and 432,000 years of man, the descending numbers representing a similar physical and moral deterioration of men in each age; the four yugas comprise an aggregate of 4,320,000 of our years, and constitute a *"great yuga" or mahayuga*.

Z

Zaebos: In demonography, a high-ranking officer in the armies of the infernal empire.

Zagam: In demonography, one of the rulers of the infernal empire.

Zagreus: The horned son of Zeus and his daughter Persephone; the central figure of the Orphic mysteries.

Zaotar: Ancient Persian for *caller*. Priest-magician who invokes the gods by reciting ritual formulas and improvised chants.

Zarathustra: See: *Zoroastrianism.*

Zehut: An early version of the name of the Egyptian god Thoth.

Zen Buddhism: The Japanese "mediation school" of Buddhism, based on the theories of the "universality of Buddha-nature" and the possibility of "becoming a Buddha in this very body." It teaches the way of attaining Buddhahood fundamentally by meditation.

Zend; Zend-Avesta. See: *Avesta.*

Zepar: In demonography, a demon, a warrior chief of the infernal empire.

Zenith: The point opposite to the nadir; the point directly overhead, through which the prime vertical and meridian circles pass.

Zervan: In an old Zoroastrian myth, the father of Ahura-Mazda and of his evil twin, Ahriman.

Zodiac: A circle or belt, which extends to 9 degrees on each side of the ecliptic. In occultism, "the heavenly man diagrammed among the stars through the division of the ecliptic or earth's orbit into twelve thirty-degree constellations known as *signs*, each with a symbol and a rulership over a part or function of the physical body." (Marc Edmund Jones.)

Zodiacus vitae (Latin for *Zodiac of Life*): An old school book by Marcellus Palingenius Stellatus, widely used in England in the 16th century. Its twelve chapters were said by Foster Watson, M.A., Professor of Education in the University College of Wales (in the modern annotated edition published by Philip Wellby in 1908) to "find their parallel in the twelve labours of Hercules," and thus "to typify the evolution of the human soul through successive stages of mental and spiritual enlightenment."

Zohar: A Jewish mystical work, the oldest known treatise on Hebrew esoteric teachings, which became the classic text of the Kabalah and the Bible of medieval mysticism and occultism. It is a compendium of Jewish esoteric thought on the nature and attributes of God, the mysteries of the Tetragrammaton (q.v.), the evolution of the cosmos, the nature of man's soul, magic, astrology, etc.

Zombie: A term originating from Haiti, to designate a corpse of a human being re-animated with a pseudo-life by black magic.

Zoroastrianism: A religion developed in Eastern Persia, based on the teachings of Zoroaster (Zarathustra). It is ethical and dualistic in that the struggle between good and evil is projected into cosmology and symbolized by a warfare between light and darkness which is conceived on the one hand naturalistically and manifesting itself in a deification of the shining heavenly bodies, veneration of fire, fear of defilement, and purificatory rites, and, on the other, mythologically as the vying for supremacy between Ahura Mazda and Ahriman (q.v.).

ACKNOWLEDGMENTS

The editor takes great pleasure in expressing grateful acknowledgment and thanks to the following authors and publishers for their permission to use copyrighted material in the preparation of this volume:

George Allen and Unwin Ltd., London, publishers of *A Dictionary of the Sacred Language of All Scriptures and Myths* by G. A. Gaskell.

Wing Anderson, Los Angeles, Calif., publisher of *Oahspe* (see p. 127).

The de Laurence Co., Inc., Chicago, Ill., publishers of *The Great Book of Hindu Magic and East Indian Occultism and The Book of Secret Hindu Ceremonial and Talismanic Magic* by L. W. de Laurence.

Duke University Press, Durham, N. C., and the editors of *The Journal of Parapsychology*.

Dr. Nandor Fodor, author of *Encyclopaedia of Psychic Science*.

Marc Edmund Jones, author of *Occult Philosophy* (David McKay Co., Philadelphia, Pa.).

Library Publishers, New York, N. Y., publishers of *Swan's Anglo-American Dictionary*.

Philosophical Library, Inc., New York, N. Y., publishers of *Hindu Philosophy* by T. Bernard, *An Encyclopedia of Astrology* by N. de Vore, *An Encyclopedia of Religion* by V. Ferm (ed.), *Forgotten Religions* by V. Ferm (ed.), *Introduction to Comparative Mysticism* by J. de Marquette, *The Splendour That Was Egypt* by M. A. Murray, *Dictionary of Philosophy* by D. D. Runes (ed.), and *Christian Science and Philosophy* by H. W. Steiger.

The Rosicrucian Order (AMORC), San Jose, Calif., publishers of *The Rosicrucian Manual* by H. Spencer Lewis, Ph.D., F.R.C.

George Routledge and Sons, Ltd., London, publishers of *An Encyclopaedia of Occultism* by Lewis Spence.

Schocken Books, Inc., New York, N. Y., publishers of *Tales of the Hasidim* by M. Buber.

Theosophical University Press, Pasadena, Calif., publishers of *The Key to Theosophy* by H. P. Blavatsky.

The Yogi Publication Society, Chicago, Ill., publishers of *The Philosophies and Religions of India* by Yogi Ramacharaka.